Study Guide & Practice Tests

to accompany

Martin • Roberts • Mintz • McMurry • Jones

America and Its People

Volume II - From 1865

Second Edition

Prepared by

Kenneth R. Chiaro
Pima Community College

**HarperCollins*CollegePublishers*

Study Guide to accompany Martin • Roberts • Mintz • McMurry • Jones, AMERICA AND ITS PEOPLE, Second Edition, Vol II

Copyright © 1993 HarperCollins College Publishers

ISBN: 0-673-53826-5

93 94 95 96 97 9 8 7 6 5 4 3 2 1

Table of Contents

Introduction

This study guide is one of several aids designed to help you master the material contained in *America and Its People*, Second Edition. Each chapter in the study guide has a corresponding chapter in the text. Volume I parallels chapters in the text that cover events and developments from the Era of Exploration and Settlement through Reconstruction. Volume II follows that text from the Era of Reconstruction to the present.

Each chapter in the study guide contains the following elements:

1) a summary of the contents of each chapter and the primary learning objectives;

2) a list of key terms, events and persons to be defined;

3) a short series of questions entitled Focus On Geography which will help you to gain a better understanding of the environmental setting of events and developments;

4) reading comprehension essay questions intended to familiarize you with larger blocks of interpretive and thematic information;

5) true/false and completion exercises; and

6) a multiple-choice practice test which reinforces the material contained in the reading comprehension questions and the true/false and completion exercises.

CHAPTER 16

THE NATION RECONSTRUCTED

Summary

Chapter 16, "The Nation Reconstructed," profiles the nation's southern, northern and western regions, during the Era of Reconstruction, that period extending from the close of the Civil War in 1865 to the assumption of the Presidency by Hayes in 1877. The Reconstruction Era witnessed the first national attempt to resolve fairly and justly the question of minority rights in a pluralistic society. The primary objective of the chapter is to sensitize you to: A) the difficult problem of reconstructing the Union and, B) the political, economic, constitutional and ethnic factors that further complicated it.

After the Civil War, many questions remained unanswered. Among these were the status of the former Confederate states and the freedmen. Quick readmission of the states without significant political and social readjustment would weaken the position of the freedmen while enforced equality would, on the other hand, create sudden and incalculable change in the South. This difficult problem was further complicated by constitutional, political, and economic considerations insuring that reconstruction would be chaotic and contradictory.

Presidential Reconstruction under both Lincoln and Johnson favored rapid reunification. Constitutional questions of legislative versus presidential supremacy, among other factors, united Republicans behind a firmer, less conciliatory Congressional Reconstruction plan.

The Congressional plan of Reconstruction called for an acceptance, among the states, of the Thirteenth and Fourteenth Amendments and the full participation of the freedmen in their political life. What emerged from Congressional Reconstruction were Republican governments that expanded democracy and enacted needed reform. Cherished ideas of property rights, limited government, and self-reliance brought Southerners to challenge the authority of the federally-backed state governments. This, in combination with public apathy and a re-prioritization of national interests in the North caused the program of Congressional Reconstruction to be abandoned in less than a decade.

Key Terms, Persons and Events

Frederick Douglass
Freedmen's Bureau
Andrew Johnson
Thaddeus Stevens

Charles Sumner
Wade—Davis Bill
Alexander H. Stephens
Andersonville
Black Codes
Military Reconstruction Act
Edwin M. Stanton
Texas v. White
Presidential Plan of Reconstruction
Congressional Plan of Reconstruction
Carpetbaggers
Thirteenth, Fourteenth and Fifteenth Amendments
Ku Klux Klan
Enforcement Acts
Redeemer governments

Reading Comprehension

1. What was the essential problem of Reconstruction as it specifically affected the freedmen and the former Confederate states. What economic, political, and constitutional questions complicated the situation?

2. What were the components of Lincoln's Presidential plan of Reconstruction? What were his immediate and long-term objectives? What, if any, protections did his plan provide to the freedmen?

3. What were the components of the Congressional plan of Reconstruction? What were its immediate and long-term objectives? What role did it forecast for the freedmen?

4. What was the nature of the Reconstruction governments? How effective were they in implementing needed reform?

5. What factors contributed to the abandonment of Reconstruction?

True or False

1. The Fourteenth Amendment defines citizenship as a basic right and implies that the states, as well as the federal government, are bound by the Bill of Rights.

2. Andrew Johnson favored the Military Reconstruction Act.

3. The Tenure of Office Act allowed Andrew Johnson to remove Senate conferees from appointive office.

4. The Congressional Plan of Reconstruction called for the division of the former Confederacy into five military districts.

5. Carpetbaggers dominated most Republican governments.

6. The major reason for the decline of Reconstruction was the belief in white supremacy shared by Northerners and Southerners alike.

7. A prominent issue throughout the Reconstruction Era was of the role of the Supreme Court in its exercising of judicial review over Congressional action.

8. Andrew Johnson shared with the Radical Republicans a firm belief in black legal equality.

9. The Freedmen's Bureau, the constitutional amendments and the civil rights legislation enacted during Reconstruction produced permanent change in the South.

10. The question of Reconstruction witnessed the first national attempt to resolve fairly the question of minority rights in a pluralistic society.

Comprehension

1. The most ardent Republican and advocate of Radical Reconstruction was _____.

2. Lincoln's approach to solving the problem of Reconstruction was known as the _____ plan.

3. The _____ Bill declared that only those taking an ironclad oath could participate in the formation of new state constitutions.

4. The process of emancipation was completed by the ratification of the _____ Amendment.

5. The most important legacy of the Reconstruction Era was the _____ Amendment.

6. Presidential military power was limited by Congress with the passage of the _____ Act.

7. *White v. Texas* gave _____ the power to reframe state governments.

8. The _____ were Southern supporters of the Reconstruction governments.

9. The most powerful institution to emerge in the South in opposition to the Reconstruction governments was the _____.

10. The _____ ended the Era of Reconstruction.

Practice Test

1. The most significant issues following the Civil War were
   a. the status of the freedmen.
   b. the position of the former Confederate states.
   c. both a and c.
   d. Indian uprisings on the Western frontier.

2. Which of the following presented serious constitutional questions following the Civil War?
   a. the status of the freedmen
   b. the problem of restoring the balance of power between the Congress and the Presidency
   c. the question of equality among the former Confederate states
   d. the problem of social welfare for the destitute populations of the South

3. In 1865, the former Confederate states would be readmitted to the Union and the terms for that readmittance would be set by
   a. the Congress.
   b. Senate.
   c. the President.
   d. the issue was uncertain.

4. Below are listed several statements about the problems of Lincoln's Ten Percent Plan:
    1. Excluded from the plan were judges and senators who voluntarily left the Union to serve the Confederacy.
    2. Ten percent of the voters of the election of 1860 had to take a loyalty oath to the Union before a state could be readmitted.
    3. States had to outlaw slavery and agree to adopt black Republican governments.
    4. High ranking officers of the former Confederacy could not vote.

    Which of the following listed above are false?
    a. 1, 2, 3, 4
    b. 1 and 4
    c. 3 and 4
    d. 2 and 3

5. The most ardent Radical Republican of the Reconstruction Era was
    a. Thaddeus Stevens.
    b. Wade Davis.
    c. Charles Sumner.
    d. Steven Foster.

6. The most ardent opposition to Johnson's Reconstruction program came from
    a. abolitionists.
    b. black Republicans.
    c. Southern Democrats.
    d. Radical Republicans.

7. Andrew Johnson
    a. envied the planter aristocracy.
    b. was opposed to slavery.
    c. believed in the inherent inferiority of black people.
    d. favored equality for the freedmen.

8. The Black Codes
    a. prohibited marriage among blacks.
    b. prohibited blacks from owning land.
    c. prohibited interracial marriage.
    d. prohibited blacks from participating in some activities if they had to travel more than ten miles from home.

9. Congress was prompted to promote its own program for Reconstruction because of
   a. the unwillingness of the South to adopt the Fourteenth Amendment.
   b. the unwillingness of Andrew Johnson to limit his use of the Presidential pardon.
   c. a determination to demonstrate Congressional supremacy over the Presidency in domestic affairs.
   d. all of the above.

10. The most important legacy of the Reconstruction Era was the
    a. Ten Percent Plan.
    b. Thirteenth Amendment.
    c. Fourteenth Amendment.
    d. Fifteenth Amendment.

11. The amendment that prohibits the states from abridging the privileges of citizenship is the
    a. Thirteenth Amendment.
    b. Fourteenth Amendment.
    c. Fifteenth Amendment.
    d. none of the above.

12. The amendment that lays the foundation for the civil rights laws of the twentieth century is the
    a. Thirteenth Amendment.
    b. Fourteenth Amendment.
    c. Fifteenth Amendment.
    d. Eighteenth Amendment.

13. *Texas v. White* declared that
    a. Congress had the power to raise unlimited taxes on former Confederate officers.
    b. Congress had the power to override any veto of its Reconstruction programs.
    c. Congress had the power to reshape state governments.
    d. Congress had the power to prohibit the Black Codes.

14. The effectiveness of the Thirteenth Amendment, as well as Congressional Reconstruction generally, was hampered by
    a. the nation's preoccupation with protecting states' rights.
    b. the nation's preoccupation with protecting property rights.
    c. the nation's preoccupation with maintaining a strict constructionist approach to Reconstruction issues.
    d. all of the above.

15. Most Reconstruction governments were directed by
    a. Radical Republicans.
    b. Scalawags.
    c. Carpetbaggers.
    d. black Republicans.

16. The Reconstruction governments
    a. were excessively hard toward plantation owners.
    b. implemented needed reforms in transportation and tax structures.
    c. instituted no significant changes in the quality of life of their citizens.
    d. were, for the most part, corrupt and inefficient.

17. Among the factors that brought an end to Reconstruction were
    a. public apathy in the North.
    b. the Ku Klux Klan.
    c. changes in the political climate.
    d. all of the above.

18. The Enforcement Acts were aimed at
    a. the Ku Klux Klan.
    b. Scalawags.
    c. black Republicans.
    d. the Redeemer governments.

19. The political party most supportive of a return to conservative government in the South was
    a. the Democrats.
    b. the Whigs.
    c. Redeemers.
    d. none of the above.

20. The final blow to Reconstruction came as a result of the
    a. Enforcement Acts.
    b. Compromise of 1877.
    c. the corruption of the Grant administration.
    d. the repeal by Congress of the Reconstruction Act.

CHAPTER 17

EMERGENCE AS AN ECONOMIC POWER

Summary

Chapters 17 through 23 of the text, collectively, describe life and institutions in the United States during the era of the late nineteenth century, that is, from the close of Reconstruction in 1877 to the outbreak of the First World War in 1914. In Chapter 17, "Emergence as an Economic Power," the authors provide a detailed analysis of both factors that created a new economic order that made the United States the world's leading industrial power. The process of economic modernization that began to transform America's material culture during the Era of Good Feelings was completed and enhanced during the late nineteenth century. The primary objective of the chapter is to provide you with a comprehensive assessment of A)the nature of the new economic order, B) those material, political, and intellectual forces that helped to create it, and C) its immediate and long-term effects on American life and institutions.

In the late nineteenth century, a new economic order emerged. The United States became the leading industrial power of the world, with a productive capability that equaled the combined industrial output of Great Britain, France, and Germany. A combination of material, political, and intellectual factors led to this transformation, which resulted in intense competition among corporations that controlled a majority of the new industries.

The new economic order enhanced the quality of life for most Americans, but at the same time, economic monopolies threatened the moral fabric of the nation, and personal relations, both within the workplace and outside of it, were radically changed.

Key Terms, Persons, and Events

Trusts
Andrew Carnegie
Drake's folly
George Eastman
George Westinghouse
interchangeable parts
Social Darwinism
the gospel of wealth
Herbert Spencer
William Sumner

Russell Conwell
Horatio Alger
laissez-faire
Adam Smith
fixed costs
Cornelius Vanderbilt
vertical integration
forward integration
scientific management
land legislation

Focus on Geography

1. Trace the development of the mining frontier as it evolved in the late nineteenth century. Locate specific centers of mining activity.

2. Where were the principal railroads located in the United States? What major cities did they connect? Which rail systems were transcontinental?

3. Where were the major industrial centers in the United States located between 1877 and 1900?

4. Where were the major agricultural regions in the United States between 1877 and 1900?

Reading Comprehension

1. The extraction of the nation's mineral resources played an important part in the rise of basic industry. Explain.

2. Technological change affected the lives of individuals more than political events or philosophical developments. Explain.

3. Who were the advocates of Social Darwinism and the gospel of wealth? What were the essential ideas associated with both philosophical orientations? How did both ideas shape American life and thought, particularly with regard to work?

4. Explain the concept of laissez-faire? How did government respond to this doctrine? Which groups benefitted most from it? Why?

5. How did entrepreneurs seek to control competition? What new management and marketing concepts emerged from this practice? How did these trends to lead to a concentration of economic power?

True or False

1. In 1900, the United States maintained an industrial output equal to the combined total of Great Britain, France, and Germany.

2. The extraction of the nation's mineral resources played a role in the rise of basic industry.

3. During the late nineteenth century, technological change affected the lives of individuals more than philosophical or political events.

4. The most significant invention of the era was George Eastman's Pullman car.

5. The United States did not rely on its native-born population for its industrial work force.

6. The strongest monopoly in America was the steel industry.

7. Political factors played no role in the growth of industry and commerce in nineteenth-century America.

8. During the late nineteenth century, government played a major role in the development of commerce and industry.

9. Free and open competition was a characteristic of the new economic order.

10. The South experienced extensive industrial growth and prosperity during the late nineteenth century.

Completion

1. _____ were legal devices developed during the late nineteenth century to unite smaller, competing firms in order to control markets and raise prices.

2. The move to the suburbs in the late nineteenth century was accelerated by the invention of the _____.

3. _____ revolutionized every industry engaged in mass production.

4. The most important development that stimulated industrial growth in America during the late nineteenth century was the rise of a _____.

5. The most dramatic growth occurred in the _____ industry.

6. _____ formulated the ideology of Social Darwinism.

7. _____ formulated the ideology of the gospel of wealth.

8. The prevalent approach of government toward industry was to adopt a _____ policy.

9. _____ was the process by which corporations controlled the transportation of goods.

10. The most significant development in the organization of work during the late nineteenth century was the introduction of _____

Practice Test

1. The legal devices developed during the nineteenth century to unite small, competing firms in order to control markets and raise prices were
   a. pools.
   b. cartels.
   c. trusts.
   d. corporations.

2. The new economic order had its origins in the
   a. Era of Good Feelings.
   b. Civil War.
   c. late nineteenth century.
   d. Gilded Age.

3. A major catalyst to America's industrial growth during the late nineteenth century was the
   a. mechanization of farming equipment.
   b. development of chemical agents used in the manufacturing process.
   c. extraction of the nation's mineral resources.
   d. development of a specialized labor force.

4. The lives of individuals in late nineteenth-century America were most affected by
   a. philosophical trends.
   b. political developments.
   c. technological change.
   d. cultural developments.

5. Drake's folly is related to the
   a. production of iron.
   b. production of petroleum.
   c. development of the transcontinental railroad.
   d. development of scientific management.

6. The most important technological invention of the late nineteenth century was the
   a. Pullman railroad car.
   b. telephone.
   c. streetcar.
   d. the gas streetlight.

7. The most revolutionary industrial development in the late nineteenth century was
   a. interchangeable parts.
   b. scientific management.
   c. team management.
   d. credit.

8. The most important phenomenon that can account for the stimulation of industrial development in late nineteenth-century America was
   a. a drastic population increase.
   b. the rise of a mass market.
   c. urbanization.
   d. improvements in transportation.

9. The rise of a mass market in late nineteenth-century America was due to
   a. urbanization.
   b. transportation.
   c. a and b.
   d. the introduction of modern media advertising.

10. In the late nineteenth century, the United States produced industrially more than
    a. Poland.
    b. Holland.
    c. England.
    d. all of the above.

11. Which did not serve as a primary labor force for the new economic order?
    a. migrants from rural areas to the cities
    b. European immigrants to the industrial centers
    c. Blacks and Native Americans.
    d. Chinese immigrants

12. American industrial growth outdistanced that of European nations during the late nineteenth century because of
    a. the presence of class distinctions.
    b. opportunities for work.
    c. fewer opportunities for both physical and social mobility.
    d. all of the above.

13. During the late nineteenth century, America experienced a dramatic migration of young people from its rural areas to its urban centers because of
    a. an overabundance of workers in the rural areas.
    b. better paying jobs in the cities.
    c. the lure of the cities.
    d. all of the above.

14. The most powerful monopolies held during the late nineteenth century in America were those held by the
    a. railroads.
    b. steel industry.
    c. mining industry.
    d. banking industry.

15. The ideology of Social Darwinism held
    a. that ruthlessness was necessary to insure the survival of the fittest in the marketplace.
    b. that survival of the fittest would develop the ideal.
    c. that poverty was inevitable.
    d. all of the above.

16. The ideology of Social Darwinism held
    a. that failure of the individual was the fault of the individual.
    b. that prolonging the lives of the incompetent through government assistance was wrong.
    c. that strong business over government and labor is both natural and right.
    d. all of the above.

17. The ideology of the gospel of wealth
    a. originated with the industrial revolution.
    b. did not espouse the work ethic.
    c. held that God sanctioned and blessed wealth and that wealth was both necessary and right.
    d. included all of the above.

18. The strongest apologists for the gospel of wealth were
    a. industrialists.
    b. bankers.
    c. religious leaders.
    d. populists.

19. The concept of laissez-faire
    a. was advocated in *The Wealth of Nations*.
    b. held that government should be involved in regulating economic growth.
    c. held that competition was natural, that the market was regulated by an unseen hand, and that supply and demand and inflation would regulate the economy.
    d. is summarized in a and c.

20. The growth of industrial power in America was enhanced by
    a. proactive government programs and legal supports.
    b. the availability of capital.
    c. popular support of ideological and cultural trends.
    d. all of the above.

CHAPTER 18

IMMIGRANTS AND WORKERS IN INDUSTRIAL AMERICA

Summary

Chapters 18 and 19, collectively, are devoted to an examination of society and private life in America during the late nineteenth century. Chapter 18, "Immigrants and Workers in Industrial America," reveals the underside of American society during the era, with particular attention to the conditions of life and work experienced by native-born Americans and newly arrived immigrants alike. The new economic order reshaped American society along economic lines and helped to create a distinctive industrial working class swelled by a pronounced increase in new immigrants. The primary objective of the chapter is to help you to become more informed about A) the sources and patterns of the new immigration, B) the contributions that the new immigrants made to America and the response of American society to these immigrants, C) the impact of industrialization and modernization on working conditions and the working class, and D) the responses of the working class to those conditions created by the new economic order.

During the late nineteenth century, America experienced a dramatic increase in immigration. The sources of the new immigration were southern and eastern Europe. A combination of many factors prompted individuals, as well as entire families, to migrate to the United States.

The new immigrants enhanced the existing labor force and brought diversity into American society. However, unlike those who came before them, the new immigrants found assimilation into American society difficult. Intellectual and social prejudices, collectively known as nativism, significantly retarded the assimilation process for them. Nativism was made socially acceptable and politically expedient through legal mechanisms, which, although detrimental to all immigrants, were particularly so to the Chinese.

Industrialization and modernization radically changed working conditions and the lives of the working class. Mechanization, as well as new concepts of discipline and management, formalized working arrangements and dehumanized working relationships. Workers responded to these new conditions first through individual acts of defiance and, later, through organized efforts directed toward legislative and judicial remedies.

Key Terms, Persons, and Events

Charles Brooks
National Origins Act
Emma Lazarus
"old" immigrants
"new" immigrants
birds of passage
nativism
Madison Grant
Jacob Riis
How the Other Half Lives
Samuel Gompers
Chinese Exclusion Act
Immigration Restriction League
Henry Cabot Lodge
quota system
Curtis Act
robber barons
Knights of Labor
AFL
Edward Ross

Focus on Geography

1. Which nations of Europe and Asia provided the majority of immigrants to the United States during the late nineteenth century? How did the patterns of "old" and "new" immigration differ? Where in the United States did the "old" and "new" immigrants tend to settle?

Reading Comprehension

1. Compare the sources and patterns of the "old" and "new" immigrants.

2. What institutional and legal obstacles prevented assimilation of the "new" immigrants into American society? What alternatives did these immigrants employ as substitutes for assimilation?

3. What was nativism? How was it expressed toward immigrants and native-born minority groups? What intellectual justification, if any, did it have to support it?

4. How did the new economic order affect working conditions and the working class?

5. How did the working class seek to resist and/or adapt to the new economic order? What legal and institutional developments enhanced the power of employers over workers?

True or False

1. During the late nineteenth century, American labor leaders sought to exclude or severely limit the number of Chinese immigrants allowed into the country.

2. America was the only country to lure immigrants during the late nineteenth century.

3. The "old" immigrants were primarily Protestants.

4. The "new" immigrants were exclusively from Italy and Russia.

5. The "new" immigrants had, for the most part, lived under constitutional forms of government.

6. The most skilled of the "new" immigrants were the Jews.

7. The "new" immigrants found it easy to assimilate into American life.

8. Native Americans were excluded from the hostility and racism engendered by nativism.

9. Notions of work and discipline within the workplace underwent little change in the late nineteenth century.

10. The first organized attempt to better conditions for workers in the new economic order came with the establishment of the AFL.

Completion

1. The _____ were the most strongly opposed to Chinese immigrants.

2. The "old" immigrants primarily came from _____ and _____ Europe.

3. The "land that time forgot" refers to _____.

4. Italian immigrants were most attracted to heavy _____ jobs.

5. Those immigrants who worked seasonally in the United States and then returned to their homelands were known as _____.

6. Those immigrants who were most strongly attracted to working in underground mines and steel mills were _____.

7. _____ was a combination of political, legal, racial, and ideological barriers that made assimilation difficult for the "new" immigrants.

8. The strongest advocate for the improvement of the social conditions of immigrants was _____.

9. The _____ became the guiding economic barometer of the working class family in the new economic order.

10. The most effective tactic employed by unions during the late nineteenth century was the _____.

Practice Test

1. Chinese immigrants, for the most part, came to America to
   a. accumulate money for their families in China.
   b. found communities for the permanent settlement of their families.
   c. flee from political persecution.
   d. establish financial empires.

2. The group most actively opposed to Chinese immigration were the
   a. English.
   b. Irish.
   c. Italians.
   d. Jews.

3. Most "old" immigrants came from
   a. Italy.
   b. Greece.
   c. England.
   d. Russia.

4. Most "old" immigrants
   a. had lived under constitutional forms of government.
   b. were Protestants.
   c. easily assimilated into American society.
   d. all of the above.

5. Most "new" immigrants were
   a. from southern and eastern Europe.
   b. Protestants.
   c. very similar to earlier immigrants.
   d. all of the above.

6. Those immigrants most attracted to construction work were the
   a. Italians.
   b. Poles.
   c. Jews.
   d. Germans.

7. Nativists
   a. opposed the influence of Roman Catholicism in America.
   b. supported southern and eastern European immigrants.
   c. opposed those immigrants who advocated the Protestant work ethic.
   d. opposed the establishment of the Masons in America.

8. The first work in American literature to expose the social conditions of immigrants was written by
   a. Jacob Riis.
   b. Lewis Mumford.
   c. Samuel Gompers.
   d. Ed Ross.

9. Nativism
   a. taught the theory of racial inferiority applied to southern and eastern Europeans.
   b. was espoused by scientists and intellectuals as well as by the public generally.
   c. opposed an open door policy to Asian immigrants.
   d. was all of the above.

10. Nativists
    a. sought northern and western but not southern and eastern European immigrants.
    b. opposed the Immigration Restriction League.
    c. opposed a quota system for all immigrants.
    d. did all of the above.

11. The National Origins Act allowed immigration based upon
    a. 2 percent of the existing population.
    b. 5 percent of the existing population.
    c. 10 percent of the existing population.
    d. 25 percent of the existing population.

12. By 1890, the federal government, with regard to Indian populations, sought to
    _____ them.
    a. exterminate
    b. segregate
    c. assimilate
    d. ignore

13. Significant economic barometer(s) for the working family was
    a. the RNR
    b. the national economy.
    c. the number of persons working.
    d. all of the above

14. The highest paid unskilled industrial workers were
    a. sharecroppers.
    b. miners.
    c. steelworkers.
    d. food processors.

15. Which one of the following did not change with the industrial revolution and the new
    economic order in America?
    a. attitudes toward sobriety on the job
    b. attitudes toward punctuality
    c. attitudes toward discipline
    d. attitudes toward profits

16. The major difference between the workplaces of preindustrial and industrial America
    could be found in
    a. a loss of craftsmanship.
    b. a decreased emphasis on the work ethic.
    c. a decrease in the size of the workplace.
    d. all of the above.

17. Workers resisted the working conditions of the new economic order through
    a. strikes.
    b. turn over.
    c. absenteeism.
    d. all of the above.

18. Government generally took the side of
    a. management.
    b. labor.
    c. strikers.
    d. industrialists.

19. The first organized effort by labor to influence the new economic order came with the establishment of the
    a. W.B.A.
    b. Knights of Labor.
    c. AFL.
    d. Workers of the World.

20. Industrialists of the era
    a. were known as Progressives.
    b. had absolute control over their industries.
    c. could not count on the support of the government against labor.
    d. were all of the above.

CHAPTER 19

THE RISE OF AN URBAN SOCIETY

Summary

Chapter 19 continues the discussion, begun in Chapter 18, of the conditions of society and private life in America during the late nineteenth century. Chapter 19, "The Rise of an Urban Society," is particularly concerned with the emergence of modern American social and cultural life within the context of the developing cities. The new economic order created the modern American city. The late nineteenth century witnessed the growing importance of those cities, not only as the sources of economic prosperity but also as the sources of a new cultural and social order. The primary objective of the chapter is to more fully acquaint you with A) the nature of urbanization and B) the interdependence of urbanization and the development of new social and cultural patterns.

The late nineteenth century witnessed the transformation of the American city. Individual entrepreneurs shaped the modern city, and the desire for profit served as the change agent in this process.

The city provided the environment for new social and cultural expression. Popular culture, in both scope and variety, assumed a new importance. Individuals, unhindered by social restraint or government control, were free to seek immediate gratification and, in other ways, to reject the social codes and moral standards of the Victorian age.

The "private city" encouraged freedom for the individual, but it also encouraged chaotic and uncontrolled growth. This, in turn, led to environmental and social problems. The conditions created by uncontrolled individualism and uncontrolled growth prompted many social reformers and intellectuals alike to scrutinize this new social institution, the American city.

Key Terms, Persons, and Events

walking cities
William Dean Howells
H. G. Wells
Louis Henri Sullivan
cathedrals of commerce
Lewis Mumford
private city

public city
Frank Norris
naturalism
realism
James Russell Lowell
Mark Twain
Theodore Dreiser
John Morrissey
John L. Sullivan

Focus on Geography

1. Locate the eighteen largest cities, in both population and physical size, in the United States in 1900.

Reading Comprehension

1. What factors were most responsible for transforming the modern American city?

2. What problems were associated with rapid urbanization? How were those problems dealt with?

3. Compare and contrast the ideas of naturalism and realism. What social conditions prompted the emergence of both ideas in America? Which literary works and authors are most closely associated with those ideas?

4. What forms of popular culture emerged during the late nineteenth century?

5. What concerns about the American city and its inhabitants caused social reformers and intellectuals alike to call for government regulation of social and economic freedom? How did this result in the battle between private needs and public needs?

True or False

1. Late nineteenth century social theory held that only lower class men committed crimes.

2. Late nineteenth century social convention held that women were unintelligent and childlike.

3. By 1900, 40 percent of America's population lived in cities.

4. The first mass transit system in an American city was provided by cable cars.

5. Uncontrolled growth was the most serious problem facing late nineteenth century American cities.

6. Individual industrialists shaped the modern American city.

7. The American city became the battleground between private needs and public needs.

8. The American city was strengthened by the social codes and moral values of the Victorian age.

9. Realism was a cultural expression inspired, in part, by the problems of the American city.

10. The ideals of naturalism challenged rugged individualism and the gospel of wealth.

Completion

1. American cities, before the industrial revolution, were _____.

2. In 1860, there were only _____ large American cities, by 1920 there were _____.

3. The condition of American cities prior to 1900 could be best described as _____.

4. American cities began to grow up as well as out because of the creative genius of _____.

5. Mass transportation created the _____.

6. Two major problems facing American cities during the late nineteenth century were _____ and _____.

7. _____ was the predominant writer of the naturalist school.

8. James Russell Lowell represented the _____ school of American literature.

9. The first individual to correlate human failures to environmental conditions was _____.

10. The focus of popular culture in the late nineteenth-century American city was _____.

Practice Test

1. The new economic order
   a. maximized individual freedoms.
   b. prohibited individual freedom.
   c. relied on government to control personal and social excess.
   d. encouraged the private sector to encourage personal and social responsibility.

2. The first American cities were _____ cities.
   a. private
   b. walking
   c. public
   d. suburban

3. The word that would best describe the character of the late nineteenth century American city would be
   a. orderly.
   b. chaotic.
   c. planned.
   d. controlled.

4. By 1900 _____ percent of Americans lived in cities.
   a. 15
   b. 25
   c. 40
   d. 75

5. City populations were substantially increased by
   a. black migration from the South.
   b. foreign immigration.
   c. migration from the rural areas.
   d. all of the above.

6. The first mass transit system for American cities was provided by the _____.
   a. horsecar
   b. cable
   c. street
   d. Pullman

7. The first critic of the social conditions in the American city was
   a. Louis Henri Sullivan.
   b. William Dean Howells.
   c. H. G. Wells.
   d. Mark Twain.

8. The skyscraper, which radically altered the character of the American city, was developed by
   a. Louis Henri Sullivan.
   b. William Dean Howells.
   c. H. G. Wells
   d. W. Louis Sonntag.

9. Mass transportation created
   a. the segregated city.
   b. the integrated city.
   c. ghettos.
   d. suburbs.

10. During the late nineteenth century, problems created by the dramatic growth of the American city did not include
    a. crime.
    b. poverty.
    c. disease.
    d. air pollution.

11. The most commonly seen and most destructive disease to appear in the late nineteenth century American city was
    a. diphtheria.
    b. smallpox.
    c. yellow fever.
    d. measles.

12. The modern American city was shaped by
    a. industrialists.
    b. government.
    c. immigrants.
    d. engineers.

13. The "private city" was characterized by
    a. the search for profits.
    b. planned growth.
    c. hindered individual freedom.
    d. all of the above.

14. Intellectuals and social reformers began to criticize the "private city" through
   a. art.
   b. literature.
   c. music.
   d. all of the above.

15. Realism sought to
   a. reinforce the ideal of rugged individualism.
   b. conform to the idealistic styles of the past.
   c. expose the sordid and deprived side of life.
   d. reject the environment as a cause of social evils.

16. Which one of the following was not a social critic of the late nineteenth century?
   a. Bret Harte
   b. Mark Twain
   c. William Dean Howells.
   d. John Wanamaker.

17. The philosophy that held that environmental factors, not the failure of the individual, created social evil was
   a. realism.
   b. nominalism.
   c. Darwinism.
   d. naturalism.

18. The ideas of naturalism challenged
   a. the idea of the gospel of wealth.
   b. Social Darwinism.
   c. rugged individualism.
   d. all of the above.

19. Which one of the following was not an expression of popular culture created during the late nineteenth century?
   a. circuses
   b. amusement parks
   c. sporting events
   d. the cinema

20. During the late nineteenth century, the American city
   a. was transformed from a private to a public entity.
   b. remained essentially unchanged.
   c. became the center of the new economic order.
   d. was both a and c.

CHAPTER 20

IMPERIAL AMERICA

Summary

Chapter 20, "Imperial America," focuses on the military and diplomatic history of the United States during the late nineteenth century. The chapter specifically discusses the roles that America played in international affairs during the era and analyses those conditions that prompted that involvement. Events and developments during the late nineteenth century would lay the foundations for American power and, at the same time, would help to define how America would use its new power. The primary objective of the chapter is to encourage you to view more objectively A) the factors that accelerated American involvement in foreign affairs during the era, B) the motives and objectives of American foreign policy, and C) the outcomes of foreign policy decisions not only with respect to those nations and territories involved but also with respect to their impact on the American presidency.

During the late nineteenth century, the United States aggressively sought to involve itself in the internal affairs of other nations. A new sense of confidence inspired by the new economic order, the need to establish new markets to absorb an overabundance of products, the impulses of manifest destiny, and a desire to emulate the imperialistic policies of European nations all helped to draw America into foreign adventurism in Latin America and as far west as the Philippines. The new imperialism emerged during the turbulent decade of the 1890s and culminated in the Spanish-American War. Many, particularly prior to the outbreak of the Spanish-American War, questioned the popular notion that America should have a greater role in foreign affairs and argued that the limits of American power had yet to be explored.

America's involvement in world affairs enhanced presidential power during the era. Congress and the public expected the presidency to lead the nation in the area of foreign affairs. Presidents of the era firmly guided foreign policy, convinced that America should have a greater influence in world affairs.

Key Terms, Persons, and Events

imperialism
isolationism
American exceptionalism

Herbert Spencer
Albert J. Beveridge
Josiah Strong
Our Country: Its Possible Future and Present Crisis
John A. Kasson
Hamilton Fish
James G. Blaine
Frederick T. Frelinghuysen
the White Squadron
The Influence of Sea Power upon History
Alfred T. Mahan
Edwin L. Godkin
Valeriano E. Nicolau

Focus on Geography

1. Locate both areas in which the United States intervened during the late nineteenth century. Which of these areas, if any, did the United States annex?

2. Locate that area that caused the United States and Great Britain to engage in diplomatic hostilities.

3. Locate the Hawaiian and Philippine islands.

4. Where were the major land and naval engagements of the Spanish-American War fought?

Reading Comprehension

1. What intellectual, political, and economic factors prompted the United States to aggressively seek to involve itself in world affairs?

2. What role did the diplomatic service play in the late nineteenth century?

3. Explain the thesis presented by Alfred T. Mahan in his work *The Influence of Sea Power upon History*.

4. What circumstances led to the Spanish-American War? What positions were taken by those who opposed American expansion in general and the war in particular? Did the war conclude favorably for the United States? Explain.

5. How did America's involvement in world affairs affect the presidency and presidential power?

True or False

1. Ulysses S. Grant sought the annexation of Santo Domingo.

2. In 1876, the foreign service was held in low esteem.

3. Renewed interest in developing America's armed forces during the late nineteenth century arose out of increased tensions with Britain.

4. Manifest destiny played only a minor role in America's increased interest in world affairs.

5. The idea of the superiority of the white race prompted American interest in expansion.

6. Among the most outspoken critics of American imperialist policies during the late nineteenth century were religious leaders.

7. Increased production without increased consumption drove many businessmen into the imperialist camp.

8. During the late nineteenth century, it was believed that national greatness could only be achieved through the acquisition of sea power.

9. The Spanish-American War was fought primarily in order for the United States to annex Cuba.

10. American foreign policy during the late nineteenth century was shaped and directed by the Congress.

Completion

1. Expansionists wanted to enhance American influence over the _____.

2. A few reformers advocated the abolition of the _____ in 1876.

3. The armed forces in 1866 only contained _____ men.

4. The most strident expansionist in Grant's cabinet was _____.

5. _____ advocated American expansion based on the idea of the survival of the fittest.

6. *Our Country, Its Possible Future and Present Crisis* was written by _____.

7. The leading exponent of American expansion for the purpose of securing new markets was _____.

8. _____ wrote *The Influence of Sea Power upon History*.

9. American involvement in world affairs during the late nineteenth century strengthened the power of the _____.

10. The most serious foreign policy crisis that America faced prior to the outbreak of the Spanish-American War was with _____.

Practice Test

1. During the late nineteenth century, American expansionists wanted to
   a. become the dominant world power.
   b. equal the European states in power and influence.
   c. dominate the Western hemisphere.
   d. dominate the China trade.

2. In 1876, America was strongly committed to
   a. intervention.
   b. isolation.
   c. imperialism.
   d. expansion.

3. Those forces that prompted American expansion in the late nineteenth century included
   a. manifest destiny.
   b. the search for new markets.
   c. nationalism.
   d. all of the above.

4. Expansionist ambitions were retarded by
   a. preoccupation with Reconstruction.
   b. fear of war with European nations.
   c. the Supreme Court.
   d. pressures from the antiimperialist press.

5. Forces that led America into adventurism did not include
   a. American exceptionalism.
   b. the desire for military bases abroad.
   c. the progressive ideology.
   d. all of the above.

6. The most ardent spokesman for American expansion in Congress was
   a. Charles Sumner.
   b. Albert J. Beveridge.
   c. Franklin Pierce.
   d. Grover Cleveland.

7. _____ did not prompt American expansion during the late nineteenth century.
   a. nativism
   b. the desire to spread American technology and progress
   c. the conviction that progress and technology means a superior civilization
   d. a missionary spirit

8. The idea that the Anglo-Saxon race must assume a role of brother's keeper was espoused by
   a. Albert J. Beveridge.
   b. Alfred T. Mahan.
   c. Josiah Strong.
   d. Ulysses S. Grant.

9. Those who advocated that America must find new markets were prompted to do so by
   a. growing labor unrest.
   b. greed.
   c. the belief that American business must either expand or die.
   d. the belief that American industry needed more natural resources than America could provide.

10. The enhancement of American power during the late nineteenth century was symbolized by the development of
    a. an organized army.
    b. an organized navy.
    c. specialized units of the foreign service.
    d. a diplomatic corps.

11. *The Influence of Sea Power upon History* advocated
    a. military superiority.
    b. an effort to establish and maintain an overseas empire.
    c. a spirit of international greatness.
    d. all of the above.

12. Alfred T. Mahan stated
    a. that naval power was the key to national greatness.
    b. that diplomacy was the key to national greatness.
    c. that the military must become more decisive in influencing foreign policy.
    d. all of the above.

13. According to expansionists, the "American Empire," should encompass the
    a. Pacific basin.
    b. Western hemisphere.
    c. Far East.
    d. Mediterranean basin

14. The emergence of an aggressive American foreign policy first manifested itself over
    a. the annexation of Samoa.
    b. the crisis with Britain over South American border disputes.
    c. the annexation of Hawaii.
    d. acquisition of the Panama Canal region.

15. America's rival for possession of Samoa was
    a. Britain.
    b. Belgium.
    c. France.
    d. Germany.

16. The decade of the 1890s witnessed
    a. a severe depression.
    b. labor unrest.
    c. political inertia.
    d. all of the above.

17. The leading antiexpansionist spokesman was
    a. Franklin Pierce.
    b. Theodore Roosevelt.
    c. Edwin L. Godkin.
    d. James G. Blaine.

18. Proexpansionist propaganda in support of the Spanish-American War was known as
    a. imperialist journalism.
    b. the patriotic press.
    c. yellow journalism.
    d. none of the above.

19. The immediate cause of the Spanish-American War was the
    a. destruction of the *Maine*.
    b. Spanish refusal to release Cuban political prisoners.
    c. behavior of Valeriano E. Nicolau
    d. belief on the part of the Congress that the Monroe Doctrine had been violated.

20. The most influential force in shaping American foreign policy during the late nineteenth century was the
    a. Supreme Court.
    b. Congress.
    c. presidency.
    d. foreign service.

CHAPTER 21

END OF THE CENTURY CRISIS

Summary

Chapter 21, "End of the Century Crisis," examines America's political life and institutions during the late nineteenth century. The chapter focuses on the national political scene, with particular attention to the political party, both as an institution and as a symbol of the new order. During the late nineteenth century, political institutions, particularly those at the national level, tended to support the status quo. The primary objective of the chapter is to provide you with an explanation of A) the values and attitudes that shaped the national political scene during the era, B) the condition of political institutions, and C) the causes and consequences of the political inertia that characterized the era.

During the late nineteenth century, nominal politics entertained the masses rather than solved the emerging problems caused by industrialization and modernization. The two major parties, Republicans and Democrats, differed little. They supported the new economic order through laissez-faire, high tariffs, and Social Darwinism, and they were more concerned with the spoils of office than the needs of the people. Political inertia bred crisis as problems remained unsolved. Although presidents were essentially honest, political corruption was rampant. In the election of 1896, William Jennings Bryan led a united segment of the population, collectively known as the Populists, to challenge the conservatives. The conservative victory brought an end to the Populist movement; however, most of their platform was eventually enacted.

Key Terms, Persons, and Events

William Jennings Bryan
"front porch" campaign
Gilded Age
Lord James Bryce
The American Commonwealth
lost Americans
"party of morality"
"party of personal liberty"
Albert Gallatin
Roscoe Conkling
Stalwarts

"Half-Breeds"
James G. Blaine
"Mugwumps"
Patronage
NAWSA
Samuel J. Tilden
granges
the money era
Populists

Reading Comprehension

1. Mark Twain was the first to call the late nineteenth century the Gilded Age. What does this term imply about the political and cultural life of the era? What evidence existed to support Twain's assertion?

2. How would you describe the national political scene as it existed between 1877 and 1900? What role did political parties, Congress, the Supreme Court, and the presidency play?

3. What was the "money era" that dominated the late nineteenth century? What were the central issues surrounding the era? Who were the participants and what were their positions?

4. Who were the Populists? What positions did they take with respect to business? What role did they play in the election of 1896?

5. What was the effect of the Populist movement on American political life? What, if any, portion of their platform was later adopted?

True or False

1. William Jennings Bryan ran in the 1896 presidential election as the "Great Commoner."

2. During the decade of the 1890s, the social fabric of the United States was rapidly unraveling.

3. Following Reconstruction, national politics was colorful but not very significant.

4. Between 1877 and 1896, several major issues separated the Republicans and Democrats.

5. The most meaningful political campaigns were at the national level.

6. Style over substance best characterized the national political scene during the late nineteenth century.

7. Political campaigns were a form of popular entertainment during the late nineteenth century.

8. Between 1877 and 1896, political power was equally distributed between Republicans and Democrats.

9. No state in the Union prior to 1900 accepted the suffrage for women.

10. The problems created by the new economic order were dealt with more effectively by the states than by the federal government.

Completion

1. William Jennings Bryan was best known for his _____ speech.

2. The era between 1877 and 1900 is known, politically, as the _____.

3. *The American Commonwealth* was written by _____.

4. The average margin in the popular vote in national political elections was _____.

5. The term "lost Americans" refers to American _____ between 1800 and 1900.

6. The Supreme Court, on the basis of the _____ Amendment, struck down state laws that would regulate business.

7. The Republicans were known as the "_____."

8. Most political corruption of the era sprang from the _____.

9. The most affected by the rapid economic and social changes of the era were _____.

10. The most formidable challenge to the political status quo came from the _____ party.

Practice Test

1. The most effective political action during the late nineteenth century could be found at
   a. the national level.
   b. the state level.
   c. the local level.
   d. all of the above levels.

2. The term that Mark Twain used to describe the political and cultural climate that existed in America between 1877 and 1900 was the
   a. Progressive era.
   b. Gilded Age.
   c. Age of mediocrity.
   d. Age of realism.

3. Below are listed several statements about American political parties during the late nineteenth century.
   1. Patronage rather than issues determined party strategies.
   2. At the national level, political power was equal between Democrats and Republicans.
   3. It was rare for one party to control both houses of Congress.

   Which of the above statements (is/are) true?
   a. 1, 2, and 3
   b. 1 and 3
   c. 3
   d. 1 and 2

4. Lord Bryce, in his *The American Commonwealth,*
   a. praises the American political system.
   b. criticizes American political institutions for their lack of respect for custom and tradition.
   c. cautions that patronage rather than substantive issues characterizes the national political scene in America.
   d. attacks the Populists for their radical political views.

5. Which one of these statements is true about the presidency during the late nineteenth century?
   a. No president was elected to two consecutive terms.
   b. All of the presidents during the era were incompetent and dishonest.
   c. Presidents were not expected to implement Congressional legislation but not to initiate their own.
   d. All of the above.

6. Which statement is true about the role of government during the era?
   a. Government was expected to refrain from actions that would affect business.
   b. Government should maximize individual freedom.
   c. Government should support the ideas of laissez-faire and Social Darwinism.
   d. All of the above.

7. During the era, Supreme Court decisions
   a. supported state laws that would regulate business.
   b. broadly interpreted constitutional questions concerning federal authority over manufacturing.
   c. upheld freedom from personal and corporate taxation.
   d. promoted civil rights and women and minority groups.

8. The most powerful political institution in America during the late nineteenth century was the
   a. Congress.
   b. presidency.
   c. Supreme Court.
   d. political party.

9. The issue that appeared to truly differentiate the Republicans and Democrats during the era was that of
   a. the money era.
   b. immigration policy.
   c. expansion.
   d. race relations.

10. Republicans were labeled as the
    a. party of morality.
    b. party of personal liberty.
    c. progressive party.
    d. party of enterprise.

11. The leading reformers of the era were known as the
    a. Stalwarts.
    b. Half-Breeds.
    c. outsiders.
    d. mugwumps.

12. The most influential political figure at the local level in urban areas was the
    a. precinct committeeman
    b. ward captain.
    c. councilman.
    d. mayor.

13. The organization that fought for women's suffrage during the era was the
    a. NAWSA
    b. NOW
    c. AFL
    d. OWSA

14. Which one of the following statements does not describe the "money" question of the 1890s?
    a. Prices dropped because more goods were produced than there was money to buy them.
    b. Deflation led to high mortgages and more money for creditors.
    c. The value of money decreased, thus forcing debtors to borrow more, and thus to demand greenbacks and silver rather than gold as the specie.
    d. All of the above.

15. According to Mark Twain, the worst problem facing America was
    a. the deflation of the dollar.
    b. public indifference to politics.
    c. political corruption.
    d. nativism.

16. Which of the following are not correctly matched?
    a. Sherman Antitrust Act/state regulation of railroads
    b. *Munn v. Illinois*/state regulation of railroads
    c. Interstate Commerce Act/regulated railroad rates
    d. Interstate Commerce Act/the establishment of the ICC

17. The Lodge Bill
    a. established quotas for southern and eastern European immigrants.
    b. sought to exclude Chinese immigrants.
    c. sought to establish laws pertaining to voter registration and elections.
    d. established stronger provisions for controlling interstate commerce.

18. The group most negatively affected by the new economic order in general and the depression of the 1890s in particular were the
    a. farmers.
    b. immigrants.
    c. middle-classes.
    d. industrialists.

19. The Populists called for
    a. the direct election of senators.
    b. the initiative, but not the referendum or the recall.
    c. indirect primaries.
    d. all of the above.

20. The Populists
    a. united Northern and Western farmers.
    b. carried every Southern state in the election of 1896.
    c. failed to win the presidency or seats in Congress but laid the foundations for future political and social reform.
    d. did a and c.

CHAPTER 22

THE PROGRESSIVE STRUGGLE

Summary

Chapter 22, "The Progressive Struggle," concludes the examination of American life and institutions during the late nineteenth century. The chapter surveys the progressive movement, an independent collection of challenges to the political. economic, social, and cultural climate of the Gilded Age. Between 1900 and 1914, Americans took actions, individually and collectively, to correct abuses and inequities created by the new economic order. The progressive movement would lay the foundations for many of the ideas and practices of the twentieth century. The primary objective of the chapter is to bring to your attention A) the nature and objectives of the progressive movement, B) its similarities and differences, and C) its accomplishments and failures.

Progressivism was not a movement but, rather, a collection of organized communities seeking to remedy injustices and alter conditions created by the new economic order, industrialization and urbanization. Progressives placed their faith in an optimism about the power of human beings to reshape their environment and their destiny. Effective government, led by experts, could provide order and stability, promote social justice, and improve personal morals. Groups organized to promote their goals and more and more of them began to win their objectives. Progressivism was, originally, a local phenomenon that inevitably spread to the state and national arena. Progressives also sought to bring order, stability and moral purity into the international community.

Most progressive legislation was disappointing. In solving problems they created others. However, they opened the door to later, more effective reforms. Their attempt to promote direct democracy enhanced the power of urban political machines. Although progress was made in distinctive areas such as child labor, there was little relief for the majority of the public. The most successful victories of the progressive movement came in the establishment of protective consumer legislation.

Key Terms, Persons, and Events

progressivism
Edward Bellamy
institutional economics
Theory of the Leisure Class

Reform Darwinism
Lester Frank Ward
Frederick W. Taylor
Walter Lippmann
Muckrakers
Lincoln Steffens
The Jungle
Robert M. La Follette
Square Deal
"New Nationalism"
"New Freedom"
dollar diplomacy
missionary diplomacy

Reading Comprehension

1. What was the progressive impulse? What ideological assumptions of the Gilded Age did it challenge?

2. How did jurists, social scientists, and intellectuals respond to progressivism?

3. Who were muckrakers? What were their objectives? What reforms, if any, did they help to implement?

4. What specific reforms were accomplished by the progressives at the local, state, and national level?

5. How did progressivism manifest itself in the international arena? What were Wilson's objectives with "missionary diplomacy"? How did dollar diplomacy affect U.S.-Latin American relations?

True or False

1. The progressives believed that experts should manage public affairs.

2. The progressives believed that human behavior could be understood and controlled, thus bringing harmony to competing interests through minor adjustments.

3. The progressives believed in universal truth and that it was disastrous to alter natural laws through human interference.

4. Progressivism emerged as a reform movement primarily from the lower classes.

5. The academic community rejected progressive ideas.

6. The progressives believed that economic competency was essential to human progress.

7. Progressivism intensified the conflict between science and religion.

8. The progressives promoted the idea of cooperation rather than competition.

9. Most progressives believed in legislating morality for the good of society.

10. The progressive movement began at the national level but had its most significant victories at the state level.

Completion

1. The progressives opposed the theories of _____ and Social Darwinists.

2. Henry George wrote _____.

3. The academic community joined the progressive movement in a revolt against _____.

4. _____ Darwinists believed that human intelligence could both control and change the environment.

5. Frederick W. Taylor held that all of human activity could be shaped and directed by _____.

6. The philosophy of _____ was founded by the American William James.

7. Oliver Wendell Holmes rejected the principle of absolute _____ in law.

8. The educational approach that stressed personal growth through experience was established by _____.

9. The religious expression of the progressive movement was known as the social _____.

10. The major thrust of the progressive movement at the state level was to establish _____ democracy.

Practice Test

1. The progressives rejected the idea
   a. of a natural law.
   b. that truths were universal.
   c. that man cannot alter political, economic and or social conditions.
   d. of all of the above.

2. The progressive movement embraced
   a. Social Darwinism.
   b. laissez-faire.
   c. natural laws.
   d. community cooperation.

3. The academic community showed its support of progressive ideals by rejecting
   a. realism
   b. formalism.
   c. the democratization of higher education.
   d. the theories of the field economists.

4. The Reform Darwinists
   a. believed that human intelligence could control and change the environment.
   b. held that reform must be placed within the confines of natural selection.
   c. supported the idea that rugged individualism had been the basis for social change.
   d. rejected the ideas of Lester Frank Ward.

5. Frederick W. Taylor taught that
   a. all aspects of human activity could be arranged through scientific management.
   b. society could change itself through planned community activity.
   c. psychological jurisprudence would bring about change.
   d. order, stability, and social justice could only come from a reassessment of the American legal system.

6. Pragmatism held
   a. that ideas were to be judged by their results.
   b. that what was natural was sociably desirable.
   c. that philosophy cannot be used to solve problems.
   d. all of the above

7. The doctrine of the social gospel
   a. revealed an underlying conflict between science and religion in the progressive movement.
   b. rejected scientific inquiry and the scientific method.
   c. adhered to the ideas of faith through action and the kingdom of God on earth.
   d. rejected the notion of sacred humanism.

8. The muckrakers were primarily
   a. journalists and investigative reporters.
   b. politicians.
   c. liberal theologians.
   d. fundamentalists.

9. Progressive reformers
   a. believed morality was a private issue.
   b. believed that social problems were the result of environmental conditions.
   c. believed that social evils resulted from original sin.
   d. were all of the above.

10. Progressive legislation was most effective at
    a. the local level.
    b. the state level.
    c. the national level.
    d. all levels.

11. The progressives believed that government should be run by
    a. business managers and other experts.
    b. politicians.
    c. community leaders.
    d. reformers.

12. Progressives at the state level sought to
    a. establish direct democracy.
    b. decrease state services and social control.
    c. protect the public by regulating building and sanitary codes at the local level.
    d. increase the level of state legislative control over the operation of local public schools.

13. Progressives in the Western states were particularly interested in
    a. taxing corporations.
    b. passing legislation to protect women and children from unsafe working conditions.
    c. regulating railroads and utilities.
    d. enacting prohibition laws.

14. Regulation of the food and drug industry, trust-busting, and a broader interpretation of the role of the federal government through the Constitution occurred under
    a. McKinley.
    b. Roosevelt.
    c. Taft.
    d. Wilson.

15. Woodrow Wilson advocated all but
    a. competition rather than monopoly.
    b. a marriage of convenience between business and government.
    c. moral progressiveness.
    d. a federal reserve system.

16. The "new freedom" was concerned primarily with
    a. moral progressivism.
    b. the Nineteenth Amendment.
    c. increasing competition and decreasing corporate monopolies in business.
    d. prohibition.

17. The "new nationalism" was concerned with
    a. moral progressivism.
    b. the Nineteenth Amendment.
    c. big government offsetting big business.
    d. child labor laws.

18. The most significant legislation of Wilson's term was
    a. the Mann Act.
    b. ratification of the Nineteenth Amendment.
    c. establishment of the federal reserve system.
    d. the Webb—Kenyon Act.

19. Which one of the following was not instituted by the progressives as an aspect of American foreign policy?
    a. dollar diplomacy
    b. missionary diplomacy
    c. the Roosevelt corollary
    d. manifest destiny

20. The event that diverted domestic reform and, for all practical purposes, caused the decline of the progressive movement, was
    a. Wilson's involvement in Latin American affairs.
    b. World War I.
    c. the election of Warren G. Harding.
    d. public apathy.

CHAPTER 23

The United States In World War I

Summary

Chapters 23 through 26 of the test trace the evolution of America's history through one of the most turbulent and important eras, the era of the two world wars that is, from the outbreak of the First World War in 1914 to the close of the Second World War in 1945. Chapter 23, "The United States in World War I," looks at the causes and consequences of that war from a global perspective and analyzes America's role in it. Before the war, the United States had been an isolated, Western Hemispheric country. The First World War changed not only America's security in its isolation, it laid the foundations for World War II, which would transform America into a world power and forever alter its relationship to the world. The primary objective of the chapter is to provide you with an interpretation of A) the nature of the global conflict known as the First World War, B) the forces that, collectively, led the United States into that conflict, C) the role, both at home and in the field, that Americans played in achieving an allied victory and, D) the effect of the war on the United States individually and the world collectively, with Wilson's failure to alter the international order through the peace process.

World War I was the first major conflict among the European powers to since the Napoleonic Wars. The initial catalyst to war was the assassination of the Archduke Franz Ferdinand of Austria by Serbian nationalists; however, underlying forces that divided the Triple Entente and the Central Alliance had been building throughout the nineteenth century. Most observers believed that the war would end quickly given that the era believed in the positive nature of progress and the sanctity of international law.

The forces that, collectively, led the United States into the conflict involved the question of American neutral rights. British propaganda and German blunders, as well as Wilson's own sense of moral correctness, also helped to move the United States into the war.

American participation in the field was significant. Wilson nationalized industry and labor and, in other ways, radically increased the power of the national government. The CPI was designated to mobilize public opinion, but, unchecked, it eventually mobilized public hysteria and hatred toward German Americans and everything German.

World War I changed American life. It ended the progressive movement. The war unleashed extraordinary fears, led to confusion among the public and their leaders about America's foreign policy. Americans rejected global political commitments and refused to ratify the Treaty of Versailles and join the League of Nations.

Key Terms, Persons, and Events

Franz Ferdinand
Triple Entente
Central Alliance
Hague conferences
Edward House
Robert Lansing
Woodrow Wilson
Falaba
Sussex
Sussex pledge
strict accountability
Zimmerman telegram
WIB
CPI
Somme
Treaty of Versailles
the Fourteen Points
League of Nations
October appeal
Lodge Reservations

Focus on Geography

1. Locate the nations of the Central Alliance and the Triple Entente.

2. Locate the Western front. Where were major battles fought in that theatre? In which of these did U.S. forces play a role?

Reading Comprehension

1. What immediate and long-term factors brought about the First World War?

2. How did Wilson attempt to preserve American neutrality? What factors made this position impossible? What role did both Britain and Germany play in this process?

3. In what major confrontations did Americans participate? What politics and practices were adopted on the home front to support the war? How did some of these policies affect Americans generally and German-Americans in particular?

4. How did the war affect political and social life in America both during the period and immediately after?

5. What were Wilson's Fourteen Points? What objectives did he have in introducing them? How did the Fourteen Points reflect progressive attitudes concerning morality, order, and justice in world affairs? Why did America reject the League of Nations?

True or False

1. World War I was the first major conflict to occur among the European powers since the Napoleonic wars.

2. Americans quickly came to the conclusion that England must be assisted in the war effort.

3. Britain seized American vessels in the North Sea despite American protests.

4. The most formidable weapon possessed by the Central Alliance was poison gas.

5. Wilson attempted to gain a peace without victory.

6. Strict accountability made American involvement in the war inevitable.

7. Wilson took America into the war, in part, to help to shape a new international world order.

8. In order to support the war, the federal government moved from taxing consumption to taxing wealth.

9. Wilson believed that the expanding power of the federal government during wartime should include control over the economy.

10. Wilson's objectives at Versailles were to establish freedom and democracy on a world stage.

Completion

1. The _____ conferences were intended to insure that Europe would not experience war in 1914.

2. The _____ consisted of France, Russia, and Great Britain.

3. _____ possessed naval superiority.

4. The most destructive weapon used during the First World War and the one whose use compelled Wilson to take America into war was the _____.

5. The sinking of the _____ turned American public opinion against Germany.

6. The German strategy of _____ compelled the United States to declare war against the Central Alliance.

7. The _____ telegram proposed that the southwestern United States would be returned to Mexico in return for its joining Germany in the war against the United States.

8. Irish-Americans supported _____'s war effort against Britain.

9. The agency established to mobilize American public opinion during the war was the _____.

10. After the war, the _____ was all but rescinded.

Practice Test

1. World War I
   a. laid the foundations for World War II.
   b. destroyed the progressive impulse in America.
   c. increased America's commitment to become more closely involved with the international community.
   d. did both a and b.

2. World War I began with the
   a. formation of the Triple Alliance.
   b. assassination of the Archduke Franz Ferdinand.
   c. German invasion of Belgium.
   d. German decision to use the submarine.

3. America became more closely involved in the European conflict over the question of
   a. free trade.
   b. impressment of Americans living abroad.
   c. neutral rights on the high seas.
   d. German atrocities in Belgium.

4. The strongest advocate for American involvement in the war on Britain's side was
   a. Robert Lansing.
   b. Edward House.
   c. Walter Hines Page.
   d. Robert La Follette.

5. The most severe violation of American neutral rights was the
   a. British seizure of American vessels.
   b. Sinking of the *Lusitania*.
   c. British blockade of German ports.
   d. boycott of American goods by the Central Alliance nations.

6. Germany adopted a strategy of all-out war because of
   a. the British blockade.
   b. the Russian Revolution.
   c. the impasse on land.
   d. all of the above.

7. The doctrine of strict accountability declared that
   a. American shipping would be searched and seized by German naval forces.
   b. British and other Allied shipping would be sunk on sight.
   c. German submarines would sink all neutral shipping, regardless of nationality.
   d. Germany would launch an invasion of Russia in 1917.

8. The Zimmerman note
   a. declared Germany's intention to sink all neutral shipping.
   b. declared that Belgium had become a German protectorate.
   c. declared that Mexico would receive those southern territories it had lost to the United States in the 1840s as a German ally.
   d. authorized the establishment of a major espionage ring in the United States for Germany.

9. Wilson took the United States into the First World War on the side of the Allies because of
   a. his admiration for Britain.
   b. trade and financial relations with the Allies.
   c. his devotion to the concept of international law that Germany was threatening.
   d. all of the above.

10. During the war, Wilson
    a. suspended civil liberties.
    b. nationalized industry, particularly the production and distribution of food.
    c. suspended collective bargaining and suppressed strikes.
    d. established boards to regulate the actions and contributions of both labor and industry.

11. During the war,
    a. the power of the federal government was significantly expanded.
    b. the federal government began to acquire most of its wealth through personal income taxes.
    c. the authority of the presidency significantly increased.
    d. all of the above occurred.

12. The organization that was established to mobilize public opinion in support of the war was the
    a. NLB
    b. AWS
    c. INP
    d. CPI

13. The anti-German influence in America manifested itself through
    a. stereotypical attitudes.
    b. hatred of German food, music, and language.
    c. mob violence.
    d. all of the above.

14. The American forces in France were commanded by
    a. Richard Yerkes.
    b. Robert Lansing
    c. John J. Pershing.
    d. Edward House.

15. The most obvious manifestation of Social Darwinism to emerge during the war was
    a. the racial segregation of the armed forces.
    b. the red Scare.
    c. mental testing.
    d. the great migration.

16. At the Treaty of Versailles, Germany was required to
    a. pay a portion of debts associated with the war.
    b. not required to assume moral responsibility for the war.
    c. surrender all colonies and to significantly reduce the size of its armed forces.
    d. do all of the above.

17. After the war,
    a. the Bill of Rights was strongly supported.
    b. unions and management reached a level of cooperation.
    c. communists, radicals, and others were ruthlessly suppressed.
    d. fascism began its rise in the United States.

18. At the heart of Wilson's peace plan was the establishment of the
    a. League of Nations.
    b. United Nations.
    c. International Conference of States.
    d. United States of Europe.

19. Which one of the following was not one of the "Fourteen Points"?
    a. open covenants openly arrived at
    b. freedom of the seas
    c. reorganization of European territories along ethnic and cultural lines
    d. self-determination

20. Wilson's proposal for American ratification of the Treaty of Versailles was defeated by the
    a. isolationists.
    b. revisionists.
    c. Lodge Reservations.
    d. House of Representatives.

CHAPTER 24

MODERN TIMES: THE 1920S

Summary

Chapter 24, "Modern Times: The 1920s," describes the turbulent years from the end of the First World War to the inauguration of Franklin D. Roosevelt in 1932. Those years witnessed a gigantic struggle between an old and a new America. Social and cultural controversy, heightened by the demise of a pluralistic society, shaped modern American values and outlooks. The primary objective of the chapter is to sensitize you to A) the great cultural upheavals of the 1920s and B) the conditions and controversies that caused it.

America suffered an identity crisis during the 1920s. Some Americans optimistically looked to the future whereas others sought to maintain the values and traditions of the past. America was no longer a land of farmers and villages but rather a nation of cities and factories. Cultural transformation was inevitable, and a cultural and social environment that reflected the new economic order began to take shape. This transformation was not painless with wet against dry, Protestant against Catholic, country against city, native against immigrant, conservative against progressive and Victorian against libertarian. The great cultural upheaval of the 1920s shaped modern American values and outlooks but gave way to the equally intense economic debates of the 1930s, which would equally affect modern values and practices.

Key Terms, Persons, and Events

segregated city
W. E. B. Du Bois
Harlem Renaissance
Al Capone
"monkey trial"
William J. Simmons
"lost generation"
Sinclair Lewis
H. L. Mencken
Ernest Hemingway
normalcy
Herbert Hoover
Ohio gang

Towner Acts
A. Smith
John Kenneth Galbraith
Carnegie Mellon
Margaret Sanger
bootlegging
the *Messenger*

Reading Comprehension

1. What forces created a clash of values during the 1920s? What controversial issues dominated the era?

2. Why are the 1920s identified as having had a consumer society? What role did this phenomenon play in changing American values? How did popular culture affect this movement toward consumerism?

3. Who were the lost generation? What values in American society did they object to? How did their work reflect those attitudes?

4. How would you best describe the political climate of the 1920s? What philosophical and economic ideas guided government actions? Who were the players?

5. What was the Great Crash? What factors contributed to it? What was its immediate effect on American political, social, and cultural life?

True or False

1. By 1950, birth control was regarded as a public virtue rather than as a private vice.

2. The social controversies of the 1920s had their origins following the First World War.

3. The 1920s saw the beginnings of urban segregation.

4. The sexual revolution of the 1920s redefined gender roles.

5. Consumerism became a new force for cohesion during the 1920s.

6. The "lost generation" were disillusioned by the collapse of progressivism in the conservative 1920s.

7. The 1920s saw an emphasis on popular culture and materialism.

8. Total cooperation between business and government existed during the era.

9. Greed and government impotence caused the Great Depression.

10. The Great Crash did not cause the Great Depression.

Completion

1. The _____ survived the conservative era of the 1920s.

2. During the 1920s, cities grew rapidly, primarily as a result of _____ from rural areas.

3. _____ restrictions were one way used to segregate blacks and immigrants.

4. The _____ took the lead in promoting racial justice during the 1920s.

5. The cultural achievements of blacks during the 1920s is characterized as the _____ Renaissance.

6. _____ redefined relationships within the family.

7. The most significant social legislation of the 1920s was _____.

8. The most significant court case of the 1920s was _____ trial.

9. The spirit of nativism during the 1920s manifested itself in the popularity of the _____.

10. The _____ were opposed to the values and attitudes of most Americans during the era.

Practice Test

1. The 1920s can be characterized as a decade of
   a. contradictions.
   b. change.
   c. controversy.
   d. both b and c.

2. During the 1920s, the growth of America's cities was due primarily to
   a. Asian.
   b. immigration from southern and western Europe.
   c. migration from rural areas.
   d. all of the above.

3. Urban segregation was encouraged primarily by
   a. immigrants and blacks themselves.
   b. zoning restrictions.
   c. custom and tradition.
   d. political machines and ward bosses.

4. The Harlem Renaissance
   a. sought to bring public attention to racial injustice.
   b. was promoted by black separatists.
   c. was a rebirth of black culture.
   d. prompted nativists to renew their efforts regarding segregation.

5. The most significant development with respect to women during the era was the
   a. establishment of the NOW
   b. securing of the franchise.
   c. public acceptance of birth control.
   d. passage of the Fairness in Employment Act.

6. The sexual revolution of the 1920s can mainly be attributed to the work of
   a. Sanger.
   b. Freud.
   c. Jung.
   d. Sacco and Vanzetti.

7. The most controversial moral legislation that was in effect during the 1920s was
   a. prohibition.
   b. the reversal of child labor protection laws.
   c. restrictions on the right to smoke.
   d. restrictions on the right to own an automobile.

8. The Scopes trial
   a. reflected the strife between urban and rural values.
   b. reflected the strife between fundamentalism and secularism.
   c. symbolized the lack of tolerance that characterized the decade.
   d. did all of the above.

9. The new nativism
    a. had little concern over numbers of immigrants.
    b. consisted mainly of members of the lower middle class.
    c. was symbolized by the popularity of the Ku Klux Klan.
    d. did not surface during the 1920s.

10. The Ku Klux Klan
    a. attracted all people regardless of class.
    b. was only a Southern phenomenon.
    c. gained political offices in large numbers.
    d. became even more popular after the Great Crash.

11. The force that acted to cohere the many forces that were fragmenting American society during the 1920s was
    a. nativism.
    b. social justice.
    c. conservativism.
    d. consumerism.

12. The most significant invention with respect to its overall effect on American life and social institutions was the
    a. radio.
    b. automobile.
    c. electrical appliance.
    d. airplane.

13. Which one of the following did not experience profound change during the decade of the 1920s?
    a. advertising
    b. transportation
    c. entertainment
    d. trade

14. The "lost generation" were
    a. writers.
    b. artists.
    c. musicians.
    d. poets.

15. The "lost generation" objected to
    a. conspicuous consumption.
    b. hypocrisy.
    c. nativism.
    d. all of the above.

16. Which one of the following is not a member of the "lost generation"?
    a. Sinclair Lewis
    b. Ernest Hemingway
    c. H. L. Mencken
    d. William Faulkner

17. Which one of the following does not characterize the popular culture of the 1920s?
    a. tennis
    b. bridge
    c. concerts
    d. bowling

18. Political life in the 1920s can best be characterized as
    a. conservative.
    b. liberal.
    c. moderate.
    d. progressive.

19. The Great Depression was not caused by the
    a. lack of working capital.
    b. oversupply of goods.
    c. Great Crash.
    d. high protective tariffs.

20. Herbert Hoover believed that all of the following should help to alleviate the suffering caused by the depression except
    a. state government.
    b. local government.
    c. the federal government.
    d. charitable organizations.

CHAPTER 25

THE AGE OF ROOSEVELT

Summary

Chapter 25, "The Age of Roosevelt," reveals conditions in the United States during its most devastating economic crisis: the Great Depression. The cultural upheavals of the 1920s gave way to the economic realities of the 1930s. The Great Depression would last until the entrance of the United States into the Second World War in 1941. The primary objective of the chapter is to help you to fully comprehend A) the devastating effects of the Great Depression, B) the policies and programs instituted by the federal government to deal with those conditions, and C) the immediate and long-term consequences of federal involvement, particularly with respect to American life and institutions.

By 1930, the Great Depression had virtually crippled the American economy, devastating millions of lives. Herbert Hoover was unable to check the progress of the depression by utilizing state and local resources. Through a series of economic reforms and public works known, collectively, as the New Deal, Roosevelt managed to preserve the public faith in capitalism and democratic institutions. Most of the New Deal's economic reforms were modest in scope; however, they strengthened the public's faith in the government as an agency of action. A variety of programs in both the first and second New Deal efforts included many people under the protective umbrella of the federal government. It encouraged people to look to Washington and, more importantly, to the president for leadership. Congress readily complied with the plans set forth by the Brain Trust academicians who advised Roosevelt on policy. The federal government assumed the responsibility for safeguarding the nation's health. For better or worse, the New Deal drastically altered the relationship of the federal government with its people, as well as the very nature of federalism itself.

Key Terms, Persons, and Events

New Deal
Bonus Army
One Hundred Days
"brain trust"
NRA
Bernard Baruch
pump priming

Harold Ickes
parity
AAA
CCC
CWA
WPA
Harry Hopkins
radio priest
old age revolving pensions
Schechter v. United States
Wagner Act
court packing scheme
John Maynard Keynes

Reading Comprehension

1. How did Herbert Hoover propose to end the Great Depression? What philosophical orientations directed his thinking? Did Hoover expect the federal government to play a roll?

2. What were the objectives of the first New Deal legislation? What programs were enacted? How successful were they?

3. What alternatives for solving the nation's economic problems were proposed? Who proposed them and why? How influential were they? What strategies did Roosevelt employ to check them?

4. Explain the particular dilemma faced by American farmers as a result of the depression. What steps were taken by the federal government to assist farmers? Why were many of the programs controversial?

5. What were the goals and objectives of the second New Deal? How successful were they? What controversial actions were taken by Roosevelt during this period? Did these help or hinder his program?

True or False

1. Herbert Hoover believed that the intervention of the federal government to end the Great Depression was unnecessary.

2. Hoover took no action to distribute federal funds to business and banking institutions.

3. The root problem of the depression was not tight credit but the soft demand for goods.

4. During the depression, the middle class became poor.

5. The status of many women rose during the depression years.

6. The first objective of the New Deal legislation of 1933 was to deal with the banking crisis.

7. A revolutionary idea of the New Deal was national economic planning.

8. The AAA regulated industrial productiveness.

9. The second New Deal sought to bring about a social revolution.

10. By 1938, the reform spirit of the New Deal was gone.

Completion

1. Herbert Hoover believed that self-reliance and _____ would see America through the Great Depression.

2. By 1933, _____ of America's families had no income.

3. The first New Deal is often referred to as the _____.

4. The first step that Roosevelt took to alleviate the bank crisis was to remove the United States from the _____ standard.

5. Roosevelt's core of advisors was known as the "_____."

6. The _____ distilled three decades of federal efforts to redefine a working relationship between government and industry.

7. "_____" would give farm prices the same position as industrial prices that had existed in 1914.

8. The most noted effort of government in the construction of public utilities was the _____.

9. The most beneficial New Deal legislation with respect to labor was the _____ Act.

10. The economic principles of _____ laid the foundation for the New Deal.

Practice Test

1. Which one of the following was not representative of Herbert Hoover's effort to end the depression?
   a. He tried to maintain prices and wages.
   b. He tried to maintain a balanced budget.
   c. He encouraged self-reliance and rugged individualism.
   d. He encouraged farm parity.

2. The essential problem with the Great Depression was
   a. a soft demand for goods.
   b. tight credit.
   c. the gold standard.
   d. an oversupply of money.

3. _____ percent of America's families made it through the Depression without experiencing real hardships.
   a. 20
   b. 40
   c. 60
   d. 80

4. The Great Depression
   a. delayed marriages.
   b. lowered the divorce rate.
   c. caused the birthrate to drop below the replacement level for the first time in American history.
   d. resulted in all of the above.

5. During the period of the first New Deal,
   a. Congress resisted Roosevelt's efforts to implement a planned economy.
   b. the president received broad executive powers.
   c. Roosevelt delayed taking action on the banking crisis.
   d. Roosevelt attempted to pack the Supreme Court.

6. More legislation was passed during the _____ than at any other time in American history.
   a. One Hundred Days
   b. New Deal
   c. era of Roosevelt
   d. Great Depression

7. During the first New Deal, Roosevelt did all of the following except
   a. take the nation off of the gold standard.
   b. close the banks.
   c. devalue the dollar.
   d. establish the NRA

8. Philosophically, the NRA and its effort to establish coordination in industry and encourage competition was reminiscent of
   a. the Square Deal.
   b. the New Nationalism.
   c. the New Freedom.
   d. progressivism.

9. Which one of the following programs was not established during the first New Deal?
   a. CWA
   b. WPA
   c. TVA
   d. AAA

10. The program that employed men to work in urban improvement projects was the
    a. CWA
    b. CCC
    c. WPA
    d. AAA

11. Which one of the following opposed Roosevelt's New Deal programs?
    a. Congress
    b. the Supreme Court
    c. intellectuals
    d. liberals

12. Francis Townsend
    a. advocated the "share the wealth" program.
    b. advocated nationalization of the banks.
    c. called for a pension for senior citizens.
    d. led the Bonus Army.

13. *Schechter v. United States*
    a. validated social security.
    b. outlawed unfair labor practices.
    c. prohibited the violation of the separation of powers with respect to interstate commerce.
    d. invalidated Roosevelt's efforts to pack the Supreme Court.

14. The Social Security Act
    a. excluded newly arrived immigrants.
    b. provided health insurance.
    c. committed the federal government to a social welfare program.
    d. did all of the above.

15. The second New Deal
    a. sought to make capitalism humane.
    b. contemplated a social revolution.
    c. attacked the idea of private property rights.
    d. advocated the redistribution of wealth.

16. Roosevelt's most ambitious program was
    a. farm parity.
    b. social security.
    c. banking reform.
    d. none of the above.

17. Which one of the following was not a serious mistake made by Roosevelt during his second term?
    a. his attempt to purge conservative Democrats from the Senate
    b. his attempt to pack the Supreme Court
    c. his determination to cut federal spending
    d. his successful implementation of the Social Security Act

18. The most significant legislation passed during the New Deal years with respect to labor was the
    a. Dawes Act.
    b. McLellan Act.
    c. Wagner Act.
    d. Sherman Act.

19. The economic theories of _____ laid the foundation for the New Deal.
    a. John Maynard Keynes
    b. Adam Smith
    c. Harry Hopkins
    d. Harold Ickes

20. The New Deal did all of the following, except
    a. preserve the public's faith in capitalism.
    b. take the United States out of the Depression.
    c. strengthen the public's faith in the government as an agency for action.
    d. increase the power of the presidency.

CHAPTER 26

AMERICA FACES THE WORLD

Summary

Chapter 26, "America Faces the World," traces America's diplomatic and military history during the turbulent years between the failure of America to join the League of Nations in 1920 and the close of the Second World War in 1945. The era witnessed the rise of America to power and, consequently, to the leadership of the free world. The primary objective of the chapter is to clarify your understanding of A) the attitudes taken by Americans during the interwar years, B) the complex origins and progress of World War II and America's role in it, and C) the consequences of the war.

During the interwar years, America staunchly maintained an isolationist stance. Memories and resentments from the First World War helped to perpetuate this position. When the war erupted in Europe, Roosevelt knew that most Americans supported the Allies but that Congress was overwhelmingly isolationist. For more than two years, Roosevelt chose to preserve the fiction of neutrality while, at the same time, unofficially assisting the Allies. After Pearl Harbor, isolationism as a popular position virtually disappeared and the public united behind the War. We joined the Grand Alliance in a popular war against aggressor nations that had, since the early 1930s sought to expand their influence. The Allies agreed on little. They clashed over everything from strategies to peace terms. These disagreements would carry over into the postwar era.

World War II had several consequences. It ended the Great Depression. The economy went to full productivity and to full employment. It accelerated corporate mergers, produced large-scale units in agriculture, and benefitted labor unions. It established Keynes's economic principles as public policy. The federal bureaucracy grew. The Democratic party would gain power, which it would hold, particularly in Congress, until the 1980s. It also increased the power of the presidency. The war significantly changed patterns of American life. The war transformed the United States from "Fortress America" to a strong, internationalist state.

Key Terms, Persons, and Events

naval treaties of the 1920s
Kellogg-Briand Treaty
gunboat diplomacy
"Good Neighbor Policy"

Manchukuo
Stimson Doctrine
William E. Borah
Rome-Berlin Axis
Anti-Comintern Pact
Maginot line
Dunkirk
Vichy
Battle of Britain
Fortress America
Lend—Lease Bill
Atlantic Charter
yellow peril
Charles de Gaulle
Grand Alliance
conferences of the Grand Alliance

Focus on Geography

1. Which territories in Asia did the Japanese seek to occupy?

2. Which territories in Europe did Germany and Italy seize prior to 1939? Which territories were seized by each nation during the war?

3. Where was the Maginot line?

4. Locate the sites of the primary land battles in Europe and the primary sea battles in the Pacific theatre.

Reading Comprehension

1. Why did the doctrine of isolationism direct America's foreign policy during the interwar years? What treaties and/or other agreements did the United States enter into during the era? With what nations were these treaties made? What provisions did they contain?

2. What ideological, political, and economic factors directed America's relations with Latin America before World War II?

3. Compare and contrast the rise and spread of fascism in Europe and Asia.

4. Why did the United States enter the Second World War against Germany and Italy? What role did the United States play in defending strategies and objectives in Europe and Asia? What were some of the more significant land battles of the war? Why were they significant?

5. What nations composed the Grand Alliance? What were the specific agendas of the leaders of each of these nations? What issues divided the Grand Alliance? How did these issues transcend the end of the war?

True or False

1. Welfare capitalism created the military industrial complex.

2. The United States refused to join the League of Nations throughout the 1920s and 1930s.

3. American foreign policy emphasized increasing America's influence in the Western Hemisphere during the interwar years.

4. The Kellogg-Briand Treaty established a mechanism for resolving conflicts among the superpowers.

5. The United States abandoned the doctrine of gunboat diplomacy with respect to Latin America during the 1920s.

6. Japan sought to impose political and cultural hegemony in Southeast Asia.

7. The United States tried to aid China economically rather than dealing directly with Japan.

8. Among the territories that Hitler seized in 1938 was Poland.

9. Government propagandists all but abandoned the effort to shape public opinion about the war.

10. Winston Churchill wanted to reshape the map of Europe.

Completion

1. The _____—Power Treaty opened China to the United States.

2. The doctrine that united the "big four" on the issue of mutual agreement before engaging in war in Asia was formulated as the _____—Party Treaty.

3. The _____ Treaty renounced war but provided no enforcement mechanisms to prevent it.

4. The _____ Policy directed U.S.-Latin American relations before World War II.

5. The Japanese invaded _____ in 1931.

6. The _____ Doctrine refused to recognize governments that were based on force.

7. Germany and Italy formed the _____ Axis.

8. Adolf Hitler rebuilt Germany's war machine in direct defiance of the provisions of the Treaty of _____.

9. The _____ Plan reduced Germany's war debt and provided American financing in the form of loans to its government.

10. Roosevelt generated a heated debate between isolationists and interventionists because of his _____ program, which initially gave financial assistance to the Allies.

Practice Test

1. The doctrine that directed American foreign policy during the interwar years was
   a. interventionism
   b. isolationism.
   c. massive retaliation.
   d. appeasement.

2. During the interwar years, the United States refused to join the
   a. United Nations.
   b. Five Power Alliance.
   c. Grand Alliance.
   d. League of Nations.

3. Which one of the following proclamations renounced war as a means of settling disputes?
   a. the Kellogg—Briand Treaty
   b. the Nine-Power Treaty
   c. the Four-Power Treaty.
   d. the Good Neighbor Treaty

4. Which doctrine directed U.S.-Latin American relations during the interwar years.
   a. gunboat diplomacy
   b. the Good Neighbor Policy
   c. imperialism
   d. isolationism

5. The Japanese sought control of
   a. China.
   b. Indonesia.
   c. the East Indies.
   d. all of the above.

6. The Stimson Doctrine
   a. called for intervention to protect the Far East from Japanese imperialism.
   b. called for increased involvement in European affairs.
   c. ignored the existence of governments based on force.
   d. gave legitimacy to the Lend—Lease program.

7. The Japanese invaded China in
   a. 1931.
   b. 1935.
   c. 1937.
   d. 1940.

8. The Dawes Plan
   a. reduced German reparations and made loans to its government.
   b. provided monies to underdeveloped Latin American nations.
   c. provided material assistance to Chinese forces.
   d. provided funds to finance American industrial development during the war.

9. Hitler's revitalization of the German war machine violated the provisions of the
   a. First Power Treaty.
   b. Dawes Plan.
   c. Four-Power Treaty.
   d. Treaty of Versailles.

10. Roosevelt formally recognized the Soviet Union in
    a. 1933.
    b. 1937.
    c. 1941.
    d. 1942.

11. The Neutrality Laws prohibited
    a. Americans from traveling on ships.
    b. Americans from trading with members of the Grand Alliance.
    c. armed merchant ships from sailing.
    d. all of the above.

12. Roosevelt circumvented the Neutrality Law by
    a. providing assistance to China.
    b. adopting a cash-and-carry policy with Britain.
    c. introducing the idea of Lend—Lease to assist Britain.
    d. all of the above.

13. World War II began with the attack on
    a. Poland.
    b. Russia.
    c. Austria.
    d. France.

14. The Smith-Connally Act
    a. was directed at labor's ability to strike.
    b. provided incentives to industry to produce war materials.
    c. provided incentives for farmers to limit the production of nonessential produce.
    d. provided for a national rationing program.

15. Public opinion about the war was primarily shaped by
    a. private industry.
    b. the federal government.
    c. British propagandists.
    d. all of the above.

16. The Latin Act was primarily directed at _____ Americans
    a. Japanese
    b. Italian
    c. German
    d. Russian

17. Which one of the following nations did not join with the United States to form the Grand Alliance?
    a. England
    b. France
    c. Russia
    d. Spain

18. Winston Churchill, through the Grand Alliance, hoped to win the war in order to
    a. reshape the map of Europe.
    b. further British colonial ambitions.
    c. establish spheres of influence for European nations.
    d. do all of the above.

19. The members of the Grand Alliance
    a. agreed on war strategies.
    b. believed in providing economic assistance to the defeated Axis powers.
    c. clashed on every issue.
    d. were able to reach a mutually satisfactory compromise concerning the division of Germany.

20. The fate of Eastern Europe was decided at
    a. Potsdam.
    b. Yalta.
    c. Casablanca.
    d. Washington.

CHAPTER 27

WAGING WAR AND PEACE

Summary

Chapters 27 through 30 of the text examine the history of the United States in the contemporary era that is, from the close of World War II in 1945 to the present. Chapter 27, "Waging War and Peace," is particularly concerned with the evolution of the Cold War and its impact on American political, economic, and social life from 1945 to 1954.

The history of the United States was profoundly influenced by the Cold War, a prolonged series of engagements with the Soviet Union, which continued until 1990. The primary objective of the chapter is to make you aware of A) the origins of the Cold War, B) America's diplomatic and military response to Communist expansion, and C) the effect of the Cold War on American life and thinking.

Between 1945 and 1954, both the United States and the Soviet Union emerged as world leaders. Soviet and, later, Chinese imperialist policies generated conflict throughout the decade. The United States responded with the Truman Doctrine, a determined attempt to resist these imperialistic ambitions. West Berlin was the first test of Truman's containment policy.

The Cold War profoundly affected American life and thought. The fear of communism led many Americans to believe that American institutions were in danger and attitudes of governmental officials increased these fears. By 1954, however, tensions began to ease between the superpowers and this easing of tensions lessened paranoia at home.

Key Terms, Persons, and Events

Joseph Stalin
Harry S. Truman
Potsdam
Iron Curtain speech
Truman Doctrine
Marshall Plan
George Kennan
brushfire wars
containment

Joseph McCarthy
HUAC
Averell Harriman
Dean Acheson
Thomas E. Dewey
NATO
the Warsaw Pact
Mao Zedung
Douglas MacArthur
Fair Deal
J. Edgar Hoover

Focus on Geography

1. Locate those nations in Europe under Soviet control following World War II.

2. Locate the city of Berlin. How was Germany divided after the War?

3. Where is the 39th Parallel? Why was this important for the Korean Conflict? Where were the major engagements of the Korean Conflict fought?

Reading Comprehension

1. What were the origins of the Cold War?

2. What was the Truman Doctrine? What philosophical orientation did it espouse toward Communist imperialism? What were its objectives? How did it influence the course of American foreign policy during the decade?

3. Explain the objectives and strategies of the Marshall Plan.

4. How did the ideas of George Kennan influence America's foreign policy? What were those ideas? How effective were they? What specific crisis emerged between the United States and the U.S.S.R to test their validity?

True or False

1. The Communist nations, between 1945 and 1954, sought world domination.

2. Russia was forced to join the Grand Alliance in 1942.

3. The first conflict of the Cold War was over the fate of Poland.

4. Truman advocated Wilson's doctrine of self-determination for Eastern European nations.

5. Stalin sought security for the Soviet Union rather than to expand Communist ideology throughout the world.

6. America assumed leadership of the free world in 1947.

7. The Truman Doctrine called for economic as well as military assistance to nations that were threatened by communism.

8. The Marshall Plan called for the economic integration of Western Europe.

9. George Kennan called for the complete elimination of communism.

10. Joseph McCarthy symbolized America's search for simple solutions to complex problems.

Completion

1. The first opportunity that Truman had to determine Stalin's intentions was at _____.

2. The conflict over _____ marked the beginning of the Cold War.

3. Stalin saw _____ Europe as the buffer zone that would protect Russia from the West.

4. The _____ Doctrine directed American foreign policy throughout the decade of the 1950s.

5. America assumed leadership of the free world from _____.

6. The ideas of George Kennan are known, collectively, as _____.

7. The Marshall Plan helped to create the European _____.

8. During and after the decade, _____ wars were fought as much for political ends as for military supremacy.

9. The Korean Conflict escalated when _____ crossed the 39th Parallel to join in the fighting.

10. _____ and HUAC symbolized America's fear of communism during the decade.

Practice Test

1. Joseph Stalin
   a. adopted a policy of containment.
   b. sought to expand communism throughout the world.
   c. was responsible for the Korean Conflict.
   d. orchestrated the Chinese Communist Revolution.

2. Truman was able to determine Stalin's objective at the _____ Conference.
   a. Potsdam
   b. Casablanca
   c. Yalta
   d. Geneva

3. By 1945, Stalin had gained control of
   a. Eastern Europe.
   b. Cuba.
   c. the Asian mainland.
   d. Greece and Turkey.

4. The Iron Curtain speech was delivered by
   a. Joseph Stalin.
   b. Winston Churchill.
   c. Harry Truman.
   d. George Kennan.

5. The Truman Doctrine
   a. called for the complete annihilation of the Soviet Union as a political entity.
   b. called upon Western Europe to lead the fight against communism.
   c. committed United States resources and personnel to resist the spread of communism.
   d. acknowledged the legitimacy of Stalin's claim on Eastern Europe.

6. In 1947, the United States assumed leadership of the free would from
   a. France.
   b. Britain.
   c. Germany.
   d. Belgium.

7. The Truman Doctrine
   a. directed the course of American foreign policy for over a decade.
   b. committed military forces to assist those nations who were trying to resist Communism.
   c. committed American aid to nations who were trying to resist Communism.
   d. all of the above

8. The Truman Doctrine
   a. saw Soviet foreign policy as expansionistic.
   b. described the conflict with the Soviet Union in terms of good versus evil.
   c. viewed the conflict with the Soviets from a moral perspective.
   d. did all of the above.

9. The Marshall Plan
   a. provided economic assistance to Western nations.
   b. was the military blueprint for the defense of Western Europe.
   c. provided economic assistance to Japan.
   d. helped to ease tensions between the United States and the U.S.S.R. by establishing a series of summit meetings.

10. George Kennan
    a. believed that the Soviet Union sought world domination.
    b. called for the containment of Soviet expansion.
    c. provided a military blueprint that included the use of brush fire wars.
    d. all of the above

11. The first test of containment as a doctrine of American foreign policy came in the crisis over
    a. Greece.
    b. West Berlin.
    c. Poland.
    d. Austria.

12. The most serious threat to American interests in Asia came from the
    a. Chinese Communists.
    b. Japanese.
    c. North Koreans.
    d. North Vietnamese.

13. The Korean Conflict
    a. was a clear example of Communist aggression.
    b. illustrated the future of American involvement in Asia.
    c. resulted in a clear victory for the South Koreans.
    d. demonstrated the effectiveness of containment.

14. With respect to American attitudes about Communism, the decade following World War II could be characterized as a time of
    a. uncertainty.
    b. optimism.
    c. paranoia.
    d. guilt.

15. Truman
    a. faced severe economic problems following the War.
    b. was successful in implementing the Square Deal.
    c. was preoccupied with labor discontent.
    d. was obsessed with the fear of Communist activism in the United States.

16. Joseph McCarthy
    a. represented the views of the majority of the American people.
    b. symbolized America's concern over communism.
    c. helped to bring about the Korean War.
    d. sought to destroy American political institutions.

17. Those who suffered because of McCarthy's actions were
    a. former members of the Nazi party.
    b. suspected Communist sympathizers in the entertainment industry.
    c. members of the Defense Department.
    d. all of the above.

18. Americans believed
    a. that the Cold War should be a fight to the finish.
    b. that communism was a real conspiracy intent on destroying America from within.
    c. that all American institutions had been affected by the Communist conspiracy to some degree.
    d. all of the above.

19. The most potent force used to suppress real and imaginary Communist activity in the United States during the early 1950s was the
    a. HUAC
    b. MBI
    c. CIA
    d. NSA

20. Americans equated Communist subversion with
    a. the rise of juvenile delinquency.
    b. the decline of moral standards.
    c. the decline in church attendance.
    d. all of the above.

CHAPTER 28

IKE'S AMERICA

Summary

Chapter 28, "Ike's America," provides an overview of the political, economic, and social climate of America during the Eisenhower years that is, from 1952 to 1960. The 1950s was a decade of sharp contrasts. While it was an era of prosperity and conformity, it was also an era in which new forces were emerging that would profoundly alter the character of American life. The primary objective of the chapter is to help you more realistically A) consider the decade of the 1950s and B) understand its contradictions.

The decade of the 1950s is seen, today, with nostalgia. The culture and society of the nation were conformist, and prosperity enhanced the image of quiet acceptance of suburban, materialistic values. This image of security was enhanced by lessening tensions with the Soviet Union. However, underlying this seemingly placid society were forces that would emerge to radically alter the character of American life. Demands from minorities, youth, and women for equality and social justice began to be heard. These demands stood out in sharp contrast to the conformist values of the era.

Key Terms, Persons, and Events

Adlai Stevenson
Dwight D. Eisenhower
Robert A. Taft
Sherman Adams
modern Republicanism
dynamic conservativism
George Meany
John Dulles
Suez Crisis
Hungarian Revolution
Vanguard
Wernher von Braun
military—industrial complex
Jim Crow Laws
Brown v. Board of Education
NAACP

Earl Warren
Martin Luther King
Little Rock
Orval Faubus

Focus on Geography

1. Locate the state of Israel.

2. Locate the Suez Canal.

Reading Comprehension

1. What is meant by the term "dynamic conservativism"? How was it implemented under Eisenhower?

2. What ideologies and issues characterized American foreign policy during Eisenhower's administration? How did these impact relations with the Soviet Union, Western Europe, and the Third World?

3. How did the desire for racial justice begin to manifest itself during the 1950s?

4. What was the image of the decade of the 1950s?

5. How and why did youth culture emerge during the decade of the 1950s?

True or False

1. The political and economic climate of the Eisenhower years could be best characterized as one of dynamic conservatism.

2. Eisenhower did not attempt to roll back social legislation established as a part of the New Deal.

3. The economic climate of the Eisenhower years can be characterized as prosperous.

4. During the 1950s, the federal government made a commitment to the automobile as the major form of transportation in America.

5. Eisenhower abandoned containment as a foreign policy objective.

6. The United States took decisive action in support of the Hungarian uprising.

7. It is fair to say that America overreacted to the illusion of success created by Soviet space technology?

8. America's image in the Third World was severely damaged by CIA covert operations.

9. No substantive gains were made toward racial justice during the 1950s.

10. The image of the decade was one of turbulence and upheaval.

Completion

1. _____ is known as the quiet president.

2. Eisenhower's domestic policies emphasized a _____ federal budget.

3. The ideological foundation under which Eisenhower built his domestic policy agenda was that of _____ conservativism.

4. The _____ radically altered the character of American social life.

5. During the decade, Americans left the cities for the _____.

6. The foreign policy approach adopted by Eisenhower is known, collectively, as _____ Republicanism.

7. America intervened on behalf of Egypt to prevent interference of its Western European allies over the issue of the nationalization of the _____.

8. The civil rights movement of the 1950s sought to, among other things, eliminate the _____ laws.

9. The most serious outbreak of racial tension occurred in the city of _____.

10. The _____ culture emerged as the first expression of youth's dissatisfaction with the cultural and social values of the era.

Practice Test

1. Eisenhower was most concerned with
   a. social change.
   b. the maintenance of a balanced federal budget.
   c. eliminating wasteful spending in the federal bureaucracy.
   d. none of the above.

2. Sherman Adams
   a. pioneered a new role for the White House administration.
   b. established a program to balance the federal budget.
   c. was appointed by Eisenhower to root out corruption in the federal bureaucracy.
   d. established the Office of Management and Budget.

3. The ideological foundation of Eisenhower's administration was that of
   a. liberalism.
   b. dynamic conservativism.
   c. progressivism.
   d. the Square Deal.

4. The Eisenhower years can best be characterized as economically
   a. prosperous.
   b. turbulent.
   c. uncertain.
   d. chaotic.

5. During Eisenhower's terms
   a. real wages rose by 20 percent.
   b. unemployment averaged only 4.5 percent per year.
   c. labor reached the peak of its power and influence.
   d. all of the above occurred.

6. The most significant changes in American social life were brought about by the
   a. automobile.
   b. jet airplane.
   c. computer chip.
   d. television set.

7. During Eisenhower's terms
   a. Americans left the cities for the suburbs.
   b. inner cities were experiencing a revival in construction and renewal.
   c. the federal government made a commitment to the creation of alternative mass transit systems.
   d. the federal government strengthened its commitment to subsidize local communities.

8. Eisenhower
   a. maintained the policy of containment.
   b. abandoned the policy of containment.
   c. sought to improve relations with the Soviet Union but not with Communist China.
   d. encouraged covert operations by the CIA in the Third World.

9. The most serious dispute between the United States and its allies arose over
   a. nationalization of the Suez Canal.
   b. the Hungarian uprising.
   c. the annexation of Poland.
   d. the policies of the European Common Market.

10. The primary objective of the Civil Rights movement of the 1950s was to eliminate
    a. prejudice.
    b. discrimination.
    c. segregation.
    d. unemployment.

11. A primary barrier to racial justice in the South was the
    a. Jim Crow laws.
    b. Black Codes.
    c. voting restrictions.
    d. both a and c.

12. The most powerful force in support of racial justice during the 1950s was the
    a. federal government.
    b. NAACP.
    c. Catholic church.
    d. ACLU

13. The Supreme Court decision in *Brown v. Board of Education* mandated
    a. the integration of public schools.
    b. busing of students in public schools.
    c. integration of private as well as public schools.
    d. the integration of all public facilities.

14. The most explosive resistance to *Brown v. Board of Education* came in
    a. Little Rock, Arkansas.
    b. Kansas City, Missouri.
    c. Birmingham, Alabama.
    d. Memphis, Tennessee.

15. Eisenhower believed
    a. that the appointment of Earl Warren was a mistake.
    b. wholeheartedly in the Civil Rights movement.
    c. that the Brown decision was not a mistake.
    d. all of the above.

16. In the popular imagination, the decade of the 1950s is remembered as a time of
    a. turmoil
    b. innocence
    c. scarcity
    d. all of the above.

17. The Eisenhower years have been erroneously characterized as a time of
    a. mindless conformity.
    b. scarcity.
    c. uncontrolled federal spending.
    d. all of the above.

18. The Eisenhower years can be best characterized as a time of
    a. conformity.
    b. contrast.
    c. change.
    d. both b and c

19. During the 1950s, women experienced
    a. anxiety over sex roles.
    b. a growing awareness of their second-class status.
    c. a substantial recognition of their professional abilities.
    d. significant increases in employment.

20. The youth movement of the 1950s was through
    a. beatnik culture.
    b. violence.
    c. indifference.
    d. an identification with the Civil Rights movement.

CHAPTER 29

VIETNAM AND THE CRISIS OF AUTHORITY

Summary

Chapter 29, "Vietnam and the Crisis of Authority," examines the Vietnam War and its effect on American society between 1960 and 1975. The Vietnam War, unlike any other before it, divided the nation. Additionally, it enhanced the disruptive forces that were activating America's political and social life. The primary objective of the chapter is to show you A) the origins and progress of the Vietnam Conflict, B) how it affected American life and institutions, and C) how it served as a catalyst for change.

The Vietnam War both confused and divided the nation. Beginning in 1954, American advisors began to assist first the French and later the South Vietnamese. By 1964, the war had escalated, and by 1968 the United States was fully involved. Americans were confused about the role of the United States in Vietnam and about the objectives of foreign policy and the political ends it was supposed to achieve. Protests over escalation of the war caused Lyndon Johnson to refuse a second bid for the presidency, and the war colored the career of Richard Nixon. Institutions other than the presidency were also affected, directly or indirectly, by the war. Congress became more active with respect to foreign policy. Reality, rather than Cold War stereotyping, began once again to shape America's foreign policy.

Key Terms, Persons, and Events

Ho Chi Minh
Richard Nixon
John F. Kennedy
New Frontier
Cuban Missile Crisis
Bay of Pigs
detente
Lee Harvey Oswald
Lyndon Johnson
Dien Bien Phu
flexible response
Vietcong

Great Society
War on Poverty
Gulf of Tonkin Resolution
Tet Offensive
silent majority
Henry Kissinger
Salt I
War Powers Act of 1973

Focus on Geography

1. Locate the Bay of Pigs.

2. Locate the major cities and regions of what was then North and South Vietnam. Where were these respective nations divided? What kind of climatic conditions can be found in what was then South Vietnam? How might these have affected America's war effort?

Reading Comprehension

1. Why has the Kennedy administration been referred to as "something short of Camelot"?

2. What were the issues surrounding the abortive Bay of Pigs invasion and the Cuban Missile Crisis? Why was Kennedy so intent on dislodging Castro?

3. What factors led America to escalate its presence in Vietnam? What role did Kennedy, Johnson, and Nixon play in this process? What was America's overall strategy in its war with first the Vietcong and, later, the North Vietnamese?

4. How was peace finally accomplished with respect to the Vietnam Conflict?

5. What was the legacy of the Vietnam War for the United States?

True or False

1. John Kennedy was the first Catholic to secure the White House and was also the first president to be born in the twentieth century.

2. Kennedy had a reputation for working effectively with the Senate.

3. The "New Frontier" dramatically altered the economic and social conditions of American minorities.

4. Kennedy did not use his powers as president to escalate the American presence in Vietnam.

5. Johnson sought to bring the full might of the United States into the Vietnam Conflict.

6. Nixon's plan to end the Vietnam War included threatened use of nuclear weapons to bluff both the Chinese and the Vietnamese.

7. Nixon authorized the bombing of Cambodia.

8. Nixon believed that improved relations between the United States and Communist China would help to bring about peace in Vietnam.

9. The Vietnam veteran was, initially, considered a hero and was well received by the American population on his/her return home.

10. The Vietnam War was the most divisive issue to emerge between 1960 and 1975.

Completion

1. Kennedy's plan for social reform was known as the New _____.

2. The most dangerous crisis that Kennedy, as president, had to deal with was the _____ crisis.

3. _____ was the doctrine that set the course of Soviet American relations during the decades of the 1960s, 1970s, and 1980s.

4. Kennedy adopted the _____ response strategy for the Vietnam War.

5. Vietnam became the laboratory for the testing of the strategy of _____.

6. Johnson escalated the Vietnam War through both the _____ of _____ Resolution and increased air strikes.

7. The greatest escalation of the war occurred between 1964 and _____.

8. The policy that Nixon adopted that was intended to turn over the responsibility for the war to South Vietnam was known as _____.

9. Nixon hoped that _____ would assist the United States in ending the Vietnam War.

10. _____ culture portrayed Vietnam veterans both as villainous and as heroes.

Practice Test

1. Kennedy's plan for social reform was known as the
   a. War on Poverty.
   b. New Frontier.
   c. Peace Corps.
   d. New Freedom.

2. The most dangerous crisis that Kennedy had to deal with as president was the
   a. Bay of Pigs.
   b. Cuban Missile Crisis.
   c. Vietnam War.
   d. formation of the Warsaw Pact.

3. Which one of the following does not describe Kennedy's personality?
   a. energetic
   b. compassionate
   c. security conscious
   d. placid

4. Kennedy was least effective in working with the
   a. House of Representatives.
   b. Senate.
   c. Supreme Court.
   d. White House staff.

5. Kennedy's greatest failure in foreign affairs resulted from
   a. the Bay of Pigs.
   b. the Cuban Missile Crisis.
   c. the Vietnam War.
   d. failure to prevent the erection of the Berlin Wall.

6. The military strategy that Kennedy employed in Vietnam was
   a. containment.
   b. flexible response.
   c. detente.
   d. massive retaliation.

7. The European nation most involved with Vietnam prior to American intervention was
    a. Britain.
    b. France.
    c. Holland.
    d. Portugal.

8. America's role in Vietnam expanded most dramatically under
    a. Kennedy.
    b. Johnson.
    c. Nixon.
    d. Eisenhower.

9. Johnson
    a. increased air strikes in Vietnam.
    b. introduced the Gulf of Tonkin Resolution.
    c. promoted an aggressive war campaign at home.
    d. did all of the above.

10. Concerning the war, Johnson was
    a. secretive and lied to the American people.
    b. counting on gradual escalation rather than a full commitment to win.
    c. unable to get the consent of Congress for a full commitment.
    d. all of the above.

11. The most serious defeat for American forces during the war was the
    a. capture of Saigon.
    b. Tet Offensive of 1968.
    c. loss of the Mekong Delta.
    d. loss of the highlands in 1972.

12. Vietnamization
    a. utterly failed.
    b. was successful in that it enabled Nixon to have time to reach an accord with the Chinese.
    c. brought North Vietnamese regulars into the war.
    d. increased the number of civilian deaths by prolonging the war.

13. Nixon hoped that the Vietnam War could be brought to an end with the help of the
    a. Russians.
    b. Chinese.
    c. Cambodians.
    d. Western European allies.

14. Richard Nixon was
    a. weak and ineffective.
    b. brilliant in foreign policy.
    c. not brilliant in foreign policy.
    d. incapable of understanding the issues of the Vietnam Conflict.

15. Richard Nixon authorized the
    a. bombing of Cambodia.
    b. bombing of Vietnamese bases in Laos.
    c. bombing of North Vietnam.
    d. use of nuclear weapons, if necessary, to bring North Vietnam to the peace table.

16. Richard Nixon
    a. feared personal failure.
    b. feared national failure.
    c. had to overcome many private and professional obstacles.
    d. all of the above

17. Saigon fell to the North Vietnamese in
    a. 1966.
    b. 1971
    c. 1973
    d. 1975

18. The Vietnam War
    a. polarized American public opinion.
    b. was the only American war to divide public opinion.
    c. kept communism from spreading.
    d. did all of the above.

19. The Vietnam War
    a. destroyed Johnson's War on Poverty program.
    b. cost more American lives than any other war.
    c. caused the public to mistrust the objectives of American foreign policy.
    d. all of the above

20. Vietnam veterans were treated by popular culture as
    a. heroes.
    b. villains.
    c. both a and b.
    d. traitors.

CHAPTER 30

THE STRUGGLE FOR A JUST SOCIETY

Summary

Chapter 30, "The Struggle for a Just Society," relates the struggles waged by women and minorities to achieve political, economic, and social equality in the post-World War II era. The chapter examines the variety of approaches taken by these groups and analyzes their successes and failures. The primary objective of the chapter is to sensitize you to A) the barriers that existed to the realization of full equality in America following World War II, B) the objectives and strategies employed by women and minority groups to overcome these obstacles, and C) the outcomes of their efforts.

The decades following the end of World War II witnessed an explosion of protest against the status quo. Political, economic, and social standards established during the late 1940s and the early 1950s were challenged, first through nonviolent and later through violent protest. Blacks, Hispanics, Native Americans, and women utilized a variety of strategies to accomplish full equality. Sit-ins, freedom rides, and urban riots were among them. The Civil Rights Act of 1964 and the Voting Rights Act of 1965 helped to break down barriers of segregation. However, by the mid-1970s a backlash occurred. This resistance to progressive measures such as affirmative action was most clearly symbolized in the Bakke case. The emphasis on Civil Rights reform that had galvanized grass-roots groups and to redefine the meaning of democracy in America became fragmented as environmentalists and consumer advocates began to join in reform efforts. The reform impulse begun in the 1950s continues, however, the results of this reform spirit are unclear.

Key Terms, Persons, and Events

Ralph Nader
sit-ins
freedom riders
segregation
George Wallace
Civil Rights Act of 1964
Voting Rights Act of 1965
Mark Delaney
Black Power
Black Separatism
affirmative action

Mapp v. Ohio
Gideon v. Wainwright
Escobedo v. Illinois
William Rehnquist
Bakke case
SDS
The Feminine Mystique

Reading Comprehension

1. What was the central issue that motivated women and minorities to assume a proactive role in reform movements during the decades following the Second World War?

2. What strategies were employed during the decades following World War II by Black Americans and, later, Hispanic and Native Americans to achieve political, economic, and social equality? How successful were they in achieving their goals?

3. What were the provisions of the Civil Rights Act of 1964 and the Voting Rights Act of 1965? What role did Lyndon Johnson play in their implementation? What were his motives?

4. How did the conservative backlash to the reform efforts of the post-World War II decades manifest itself legally, politically, economically, and socially?

5. What role did women and youth play in the reform movements of the contemporary era? How did these movements compare in strategy and objectives to those seeking racial equality? What specific issues concern the feminist movement today? Has feminism redefined American values? How?

True or False

1. The reform spirit of the post-World War II era was the manifestation of a grass-roots political movement.

2. The focus of Black protest in contemporary America has been on the elimination of segregation.

3. The search for racial equality was primarily contained to an attempt to modify legal and social practices in the South.

4. John Kennedy had little passion for the cause of racial equality.

5. The Voting Rights Act of 1965 overrode state constitutional limitations specifically aimed at Black voter participation.

6. The youth movement symbolized a growing generation gap in the United States.

7. The Equal pay Act of 1963 was the first federal legislation to deal with the issue of discrimination on the basis of sex.

8. The most controversial Supreme Court decision handed down during the 1970s was *Roe v. Wade*.

9. Organized labor helped to defeat the passage of the ERA.

10. By 1990, women and minorities had made no gains in political, economic, and social equality.

Completion

1. The most significant person in the consumer movement of the 1970s and 1980s was _____.

2. The catalyst to the reform movement of the post-World War II decades was the search for racial _____.

3. The first group to renounce the legalistic approach to the eradication of inequality was _____.

4. President _____ played the most significant role in bringing about the Civil Rights Act of 1964.

5. Martin Delaney advocated black _____.

6. The most vocal group in the youth movement was the _____.

7. The doctrine that caused a conservative backlash to the reform movements begun in the mid-1950s was _____.

8. Today, only 2 percent of the nation's officeholders are _____.

9. _____ revolutionized the women's movement.

10. The most vocal movement that has sought to resist the growing influence of feminism has been the right to _____ movement.

Practice Test

1. Ralph Nader was responsible for all of the following except the
   a. National Traffic Motor Vehicle Safety Act.
   b. OSHA.
   c. Consumer Product Safety Act.
   d. Civil Rights Act.

2. The activism of the 1960s
   a. stressed a reemphasis on American democracy and the improvement of the quality of life.
   b. fought nativism.
   c. espoused materialism.
   d. stressed the adoption of a new nationalism.

3. All of the following strategies were used to gain racial justice except
   a. federal legislation.
   b. sit-ins.
   c. violence.
   d. migration.

4. The first Black to enter a post-secondary institution in the South was
   a. George Wallace.
   b. James Meredith.
   c. Mark Delaney.
   d. Martin Luther King, Jr.

5. Reforms of the post-World War II era fought against
   a. segregation.
   b. police brutality.
   c. job discrimination.
   d. all of the above.

6. The Civil Rights Act of 1964 did all of the following except
   a. prohibit discrimination in voting practices.
   b. prohibit discrimination in employment.
   c. prohibit discrimination in the use of public facilities.
   d. establish the EEOC.

7. The Black Muslims
   a. believed that prayer and meditation would lead to full racial justice.
   b. advocated Black separatism.
   c. used only nonviolent means of protest.
   d. did not participate in the reform movement.

8. Lyndon Johnson did all of the following except
   a. promote the Fair Housing Act.
   b. support the War on Poverty.
   c. supported the Civil Rights Act of 1964.
   d. supported strict constructionist interpretations of the Constitution.

9. Lyndon Johnson
   a. appointed the first Black man to the federal bench.
   b. appointed the first Black woman to the Supreme Court.
   c. instituted, through Congress, the Affirmative Action Plan.
   d. did all of the above.

10. The conservative "backlash" to the reform movement manifested itself in all but which of the following?
    a. white flight
    b. loose constructionist interpretations of Civil Rights legislation by the Supreme Court
    c. the emergence of George Wallace as a Presidential candidate
    d. attempts to rescind the Fair Housing and Voting Rights acts

11. *Mapp v. Ohio* required that
    a. defendants prove that the police had refused the presence of an attorney during questioning.
    b. an attorney be appointed for all defendants.
    c. evidence secured through unreasonable searches must be excluded.
    d. a defendant's rights be read to him or her prior to arrest and questioning.

12. During the 1970s, the most controversial Supreme Court decision pertaining to racial justice was the
    a. Bakke case.
    b. Weber case.
    c. Miranda case.
    d. Mapp case.

13. Today, Blacks hold less than _____ percent of public offices.
    a. 0
    b. 2
    c. 10
    d. 25

14. The most vocal groups associated with the youth revolt was
    a. the SDS.
    b. the SUO.
    c. the NOW.
    d. none of the above.

15. The youth revolt was marked by all of the following except
    a. skepticism about the values and ambitions reflected in the suburban culture.
    b. identification with injustice for others.
    c. contempt for the economic order.
    d. a desire to foster a generation gap.

16. Some of the literature of social activism of the era included
    a. *Catcher in the Rye*.
    b. *Rebel Without a Cause*.
    c. *The Feminine Mystique*.
    d. *The Grapes of Wrath*.

17. Sources of female discontent during the era included
    a. a concern about their lack of political power and influence.
    b. a concern about the inequality of women as a working group.
    c. concerns about reproductive rights.
    d. all of the above.

18. The most significant Supreme Court decision concerning the rights of women during the 1970s was
    a. *Roe v. Wade*.
    b. *Mapp v. Ohio*.
    c. *Gideon v. Wainwright*.
    d. *Escobedo v. Illinois*.

19. The group that appears to have gained the least amount of advantage from the reform movement of the post-World War II decades are
    a. women.
    b. Blacks.
    c. Hispanics.
    d. Native Americans.

20. The conservative grass-roots reaction to the reform movements of the era include
    a. reverse discrimination.
    b. antiabortion.
    c. strict constructionist interpretations of defendant's rights.
    d. a return to laissez-faire.

CHAPTER 31

AMERICA IN OUR TIME

Summary

Chapter 31, "America in Our Time," summarizes events and developments in the nation's history from the election of Richard Nixon to his second presidential term in 1972 to the present. The chapter discusses these events and develops them within the context of the Watergate scandal. The Watergate scandal not only ended Nixon's presidential career but also ended the dominion of the imperial presidency. The primary objective of the chapter is to help you to more clearly understand A) the present conditions of American life and institutions and B) the forces that helped to shape them.

America at the end of the twentieth century is a paradox. As the century draws to a close, American ideas of freedom and democracy are ascendant. Despite the influx of foreign competition, America remains the leading industrial nation of the world. However, after a century and a half of social experimentation of one type or another, America has not been able to eradicate social evils and injustices. Successes in foreign policy, particularly the winning of the Cold War and the Gulf War, have reaffirmed Americans' confidence in their foreign policy objectives. However, concerns about the growing national debt and the uncertain economic future appear to offset these optimistic views.

Key Terms, Persons, and Events

Watergate
Houston Plan
"plumbers"
imperial presidency
John Dean
Daniel Ellsberg
Archibald Cox
executive privilege
Jimmy Carter
Gerald Ford
Lee Iacocca
Leonid Brezhnev
New Federalism
Ronald Reagan

Iran Gate
Glasnost
Perestroika
Desert Storm
James Baker
George Bush

Focus on Geography

1. How did the collapse of communism affect the political geography of Eastern Europe and other areas of the Soviet Union?

2. Locate Iraq and its principle cities and regions.

Reading Comprehension

1. Watergate posed a grave threat to the constitutional system of the United States. Explain both how and why.

2. How did Congress respond to Watergate? Have these actions been effective?

3. Compare and contrast the Ford and Carter administrations in terms of strengths, weaknesses, accomplishments, and failures.

4. The integration of foreign causes into American economic troubles appears to be prevalent. Explain.

5. What factors contributed to the end of the Cold War? How influential was the United States in that process?

True or False

1. Watergate posed a grave threat to the American constitutional system.

2. Watergate returned a balance of power between the legislative and executive branches.

3. The War Powers Act of 1973 has not been evoked.

4. Both Carter and Ford established strong energy and environmental policies.

5. The major competitor to American industrial productivity is Japan.

6. By 1990, many Americans were spending 50 percent and more of their monthly incomes for housing.

7. The integration of foreign political and economic action causes American economic problems.

8. The major cause of American concern in foreign policy has been the failure to control international terrorism.

9. Reagan revolutionized public policy through the introduction of the New Federalism.

10. At present, American ideas of freedom and democracy are ascendant.

Completion

1. Instrumental in the Watergate break-in were the "_____."

2. The _____ Plan was intended to humiliate and discredit democratic candidates in the 1972 presidential and congressional elections.

3. The strength of the presidency has, over time, come primarily from the doctrine of _____ privilege.

4. The imperial presidency began when _____ significantly increased presidential powers.

5. The problems of _____ and high interest rates troubled both the Carter and Ford administrations.

6. The most visible symbol of American economic success today is _____.

7. _____ controls the majority of the world's oil supply.

8. The first challenge that tested Reagan's abilities as president was the _____ strike.

9. "_____" means the liberalization of the Soviet political system.

10. "_____" refers to recent economic reforms throughout the former Soviet Union.

Practice Test

1. The most serious threat to the constitutional system of the United States was the
   a. Vietnam War.
   b. SDS.
   c. assassination of Martin Luther King, Jr.
   d. Watergate incident.

2. Watergate resulted in
   a. a substantial gain in the power and prestige of Congress.
   b. a lack of public respect for the office of the presidency.
   c. the elimination of executive privilege.
   d. the formation of an oversight committee of Congress to review presidential decisions.

3. The imperial presidency, with its legislative agenda and extensive power, began with
   a. Woodrow Wilson.
   b. Theodore Roosevelt.
   c. Franklin D. Roosevelt.
   d. John Kennedy.

4. Watergate resulted in
   a. the establishment of a national Freedom Information Act.
   b. a modified filibuster process in the Senate.
   c. a weakened seniority system in the House.
   d. all of the above.

5. Gerald Ford and Jimmy Carter
   a. were honest but not dynamic.
   b. worked extremely well with Congress.
   c. had effective foreign policies.
   d. were all of the above.

6. Gerald Ford was opposed primarily by the
   a. moderate wing of the Democratic party.
   b. liberal caucus in Congress.
   c. conservative Republican party members and members of Congress.
   d. liberal wing of the Republican party.

7. Both the Carter and Ford administrations were hindered in their effectiveness by
   a. rising inflation.
   b. rising interest rates.
   c. both a and b.
   d. recession.

8. The most obvious symbol of American economic success today is
   a. George Bush.
   b. Ross Perot.
   c. Lee Iacocca.
   d. Mario Cuomo.

9. The most serious economic crisis of the 1970s dealt with a shortage of
   a. oil.
   b. nuclear power.
   c. raw materials.
   d. markets for American goods.

10. During the 1970s, America was a hostage to the whims of
    a. the League of Arab States.
    b. OPEC.
    c. the Common Market.
    d. the Organization of American States.

11. The cause(s) of American economic stagnation include
    a. the economic and political actions of foreign nations.
    b. rapid deflation.
    c. the local deficit.
    d. all of the above.

12. Americans today may spend _____ percent of their monthly income.
    a. 25
    b. 33
    c. 50
    d. 75

13. The most serious threat to American economic leadership in the world comes from
    a. Japan.
    b. Communist China.
    c. Great Britain.
    d. the Organization of American States.

14. Which one of the following does not characterize America's economy today?
    a. flattening wages
    b. rising prices
    c. reactive to world conditions
    d. deflation

15. The doctrine that characterized Soviet-American relations during the 1970s and 1980s was
    a. containment.
    b. massive retaliation.
    c. Glasnost
    d. detente.

16. Jimmy Carter's presidency was severely damaged by the
    a. capture of the *Mayaguez*.
    b. fall of the Shah of Iran.
    c. taking of American hostages by Iranian fundamentalists.
    d. hijacking of commercial airlines.

17. The most serious threat to international security and order has been
    a. terrorism.
    b. the threat of the use of nuclear weapons by the superpowers.
    c. the rise of international violence.
    d. the failure of the United Nations.

18. Reagan
    a. strongly supported Civil Rights legislation.
    b. balanced the federal budget.
    c. returned to the practice of containment in foreign policy.
    d. advocated supply side economics.

19. The liberaliation of the Soviet political system is known as
    a. Glasnost.
    b. Perestroika.
    c. detente.
    d. openness.

20. The economic reform of the Soviet political system is known as
    a. Glasnost.
    b. Perestroika.
    c. detente.
    d. openness.

CHAPTER 16

True/False
1. T
2. F
3. F
4. T
5. T
6. T
7. F
8. F
9. F
10. T

Completion
1. Thaddeus Stevens
2. Ten Percent
3. Wade-Davis
4. Thirteenth
5. Fourteenth
6. Commander of the Army
7. Congress
8. scalawags
9. Ku Klux Klan
10. Compromise of 1877

Practice Test
1. C
2. B
3. C
4. C
5. A
6. D
7. C
8. C
9. D
10. C
11. B
12. B
13. C
14. D
15. C
16. B
17. D
18. A
19. A
20. B

CHAPTER 17

True/False
1. T
2. T
3. T
4. F
5. T
6. F
7. F
8. F
9. F
10. F

Completion
1. Trusts
2. streetcar
3. Interchangeable parts
4. mass market
5. food processing
6. Herbert Spencer
7. Andrew Carnegie
8. laissez-faire
9. Forward integration
10. scientific management

Practice Test
1. C
2. A
3. C
4. C
5. B
6. B
7. A
8. B
9. C
10. C
11. C
12. B
13. D
14. A
15. D
16. D
17. C
18. C
19. D
20. D

CHAPTER 18

True/False
1. T
2. F
3. T
4. F
5. F
6. T
7. F
8. F
9. F
10. F

Completion
1. Irish
2. northern, western
3. Italy
4. construction
5. birds of passage
6. Poles
7. Nativism
8. Jacob Riis
9. family economy
10. strike

Practice Test
1. A
2. B
3. C
4. D
5. A
6. A
7. A
8. A
9. D
10. A
11. A
12. C
13. C
14. B
15. D
16. B
17. D
18. A
19. A
20. D

CHAPTER 19

True/False
1. F
2. T
3. T
4. F
5. T
6. T
7. T
8. F
9. T
10. T

Completion
1. walking cities
2. 9, 68
3. chaotic
4. Louis Henri Sullivan
5. segregated city
6. crime, disease
7. Frank Norris
8. realist
9. Theodore Dreiser
10. entertainment

Practice Test
1. A
2. B
3. B
4. C
5. D
6. A
7. B
8. A
9. A
10. D
11. C
12. A
13. D
14. D
15. C
16. D
17. D
18. D
19. D
20. D

CHAPTER 20

True/False
1. T
2. T
3. F
4. F
5. T
6. F
7. T
8. T
9. F
10. F

Completion
1. Western Hemisphere
2. foreign service
3. 11,000
4. William Seward
5. Social Darwinists
6. Josiah Strong
7. John Kasson
8. Alfred T. Mahon
9. Presidency
10. Britain

Practice Test
1. C
2. B
3. D
4. A
5. D
6. B
7. A
8. C
9. C
10. B
11. B
12. A
13. B
14. A
15. D
16. D
17. C
18. C
19. A
20. C

CHAPTER 21

True/False
1. T
2. T
3. T
4. F
5. F
6. T
7. T
8. T
9. F
10. T

Completion
1. Cross of Gold
2. Gilded Age
3. Lord Bryce
4. 1.5 percent
5. presidents
6. Fourteenth
7. party of morality
8. spoils system
9. farmers
10. Populist

Practice Test
1. C
2. B
3. A
4. C
5. D
6. D
7. C
8. D
9. B
10. A
11. D
12. B
13. A
14. D
15. C
16. A
17. C
18. A
19. A
20. A

CHAPTER 22

True/False
1. T
2. T
3. F
4. F
5. T
6. T
7. F
8. T
9. T
10. F

Completion
1. natural law
2. *Progress and Poverty*
3. formalism
4. Reform
5. scientific management
6. pragmatism
7. truth
8. John Dewey
9. gospel
10. direct

Practice Test
1. D
2. D
3. B
4. A
5. A
6. A
7. C
8. A
9. B
10. D
11. A
12. A
13. A
14. B
15. B
16. C
17. C
18. C
19. D
20. B

CHAPTER 23

True/False
1. T
2. F
3. T
4. F
5. T
6. T
7. T
8. T
9. F
10. T

Completion
1. Hague
2. Triple Entente
3. Britain
4. submarine
5. *Lusitania*
6. strict accountability
7. Zimmerman
8. Germany's, Britain
9. CPI
10. Bill of Rights

Practice Test
1. D
2. B
3. C
4. C
5. B
6. B
7. C
8. C
9. D
10. D
11. D
12. D
13. D
14. C
15. D
16. C
17. C
18. A
19. C
20. A

CHAPTER 24

True/False
1. T
2. F
3. F
4. F
5. T
6. F
7. T
8. T
9. T
10. T

Completion
1. progressive
2. immigration
3. Zoning
4. Urban League
5. Harlem
6. Birth control
7. prohibition
8. Scopes
9. Ku Klux Klan
10. lost generation

Practice Test
1. D
2. C
3. B
4. C
5. C
6. B
7. A
8. D
9. C
10. C
11. D
12. B
13. B
14. A
15. D
16. D
17. C
18. A
19. C
20. C

CHAPTER 25

True/False
1. T
2. F
3. T
4. T
5. T
6. T
7. T
8. F
9. F
10. T

Completion
1. rugged individualism
2. one-fourth
3. One Hundred Days
4. gold
5. Brain Trust
6. NRA
7. Parity
8. TVA
9. Wagner
10. John Maynard Keynes

Practice Test
1. D
2. A
3. B
4. D
5. B
6. A
7. D
8. B
9. B
10. A
11. B
12. C
13. C
14. C
15. A
16. B
17. D
18. C
19. A
20. B

CHAPTER 26

True/False
1. F
2. T
3. T
4. F
5. T
6. T
7. T
8. F
9. T
10. T

Completion
1. Nine
2. Four
3. Kellogg-Briand
4. Good Neighbor
5. Manchuria
6. Stimson
7. Rome-Berlin
8. Versailles
9. Dawes
10. Lend—Lease

Practice Test
1. B
2. D
3. A
4. B
5. D
6. C
7. C
8. A
9. D
10. A
11. C
12. D
13. A
14. A
15. A
16. A
17. D
18. D
19. C
20. B

CHAPTER 27

True/False
1. T
2. T
3. T
4. T
5. F
6. T
7. T
8. T
9. F
10. T

Completion
1. Potsdam
2. Poland
3. Eastern
4. Truman
5. Britain
6. containment
7. Common Market
8. brushfire
9. China
10. McCarthy

Practice Test
1. B
2. A
3. A
4. B
5. C
6. B
7. D
8. D
9. A
10. D
11. B
12. A
13. B
14. C
15. A
16. B
17. B
18. D
19. A
20. D

CHAPTER 28

True/False
1. T
2. T
3. T
4. T
5. F
6. F
7. T
8. T
9. F
10. F

Completion
1. Eisenhower
2. balanced
3. dynamic
4. automobile
5. suburbs
6. dominant
7. Suez Canal
8. Jim Crow
9. Little Rock, Arkansas
10. beatnik

Practice Test
1. B
2. A
3. B
4. A
5. D
6. A
7. A
8. A
9. A
10. C
11. D
12. B
13. A
14. A
15. A
16. B
17. A
18. D
19. A
20. A

CHAPTER 29

True/False
1. T
2. F
3. F
4. F
5. F
6. F
7. T
8. T
9. F
10. T

Completion
1. Frontier
2. Cuban Missile
3. Detente
4. flexible
5. counterinsurgency
6. Gulf, Tonkin
7. 1968
8. Vietnamization
9. China
10. Popular

Practice Test
1. B
2. B
3. D
4. B
5. A
6. B
7. B
8. B
9. D
10. B
11. B
12. A
13. B
14. B
15. A
16. D
17. D
18. A
19. C
20. C

CHAPTER 30

True/False
1. T
2. T
3. F
4. F
5. F
6. T
7. T
8. T
9. T
10. F

Completion
1. Ralph Nader
2. justice
3. CORE
4. Lyndon Johnson
5. separatism
6. SDS
7. affirmative action
8. Black
9. *The Feminine Mystique*
10. life

Practice Test
1. D
2. D
3. D
4. B
5. D
6. A
7. B
8. D
9. C
10. B
11. C
12. A
13. B
14. A
15. D
16. C
17. D
18. A
19. D
20. D

CHAPTER 31

True/False

1. T
2. T
3. T
4. F
5. T
6. T
7. T
8. T
9. T
10. T

Completion

1. plumbers
2. Huston
3. executive
4. Theodore Roosevelt
5. inflation
6. Lee Iacocca
7. OPEC
8. air traffic controllers strike
9. Glasnost
10. Perestroika

Practice Test

1. D
2. A
3. B
4. D
5. A
6. C
7. C
8. C
9. A
10. B
11. A
12. C
13. A
14. D
15. D
16. C
17. A
18. D
19. A
20. B